War Music

WAR
MUSIC

An Account
of Books 1–4 and 16–19
of Homer's *Iliad*

Christopher Logue

The University of Chicago Press

Published by arrangement with Farrar, Straus, and Giroux, LLC

The University of Chicago Press, Chicago, 60637
Copyright © 1997 by Christopher Logue
All rights reserved. First published 1997
University of Chicago Press edition 2003

The three books in this volume were published in Britain and by Farrar, Straus, and Giroux as *Kings* (Faber and Faber, Ltd., 1991/FSG, 1991), *The Husbands* (Faber and Faber, Ltd., 1994/FSG, 1995), and *War Music* (Jonathan Cape, Ltd., 1981/FSG, 1987).

Printed in the United States of America

12 11 10 09 08 07   3 4 5

Library of Congress Cataloging-in-Publication Data

Logue, Christopher, 1926–
        War music : an account of books 1–4 and 16–19 of Homer's Iliad /
    Christopher Logue.—University of Chicago Press ed.
            p.   cm.
        Contents: Kings — The husbands — War music.
        ISBN 0-226-49190-0 (alk. paper)
            1. Achilles (Greek mythology)—Poetry.   2. Epic poetry, Greek—
    Adaptations.   3. Trojan War—Poetry.   4. Homer—Adaptations.
    I. Homer. Iliad. Book 1–4.   II. Homer. Iliad. Book 16–19.
    III. Title.

    PR6023 .O38W36 2003
    821'.914—dc21

                                                        2003051357

♾ The paper used in this publication meets the minimum requirements of the American National Standard for Information Sciences—Permanence of Paper for Printed Library Materials, ANSI Z39.48-1992.

Contents

Author's Note

Either the translations of the *Iliad* on which the three parts of *War Music* are based did not exist or they had had only a passing interest for me until 1959, when Donald Carne-Ross suggested I contribute to a new version of the poem he was about to commission for the BBC.

Knowing no Greek, I began work on the passage he chose for me by studying the same passage in the translations published by Chapman (1611), Pope (1720), Lord Derby (1865), A. T. Murray (1924), and Rieu (1950).

While Pope was the most and Murray the least accomplished of these authors, Murray, according to learned gossip, possessed the most and Pope the least information about Homer's Greek—though Chapman had tried to abort the charge that his translation was based on a French crib by calling his judges "envious Windfuckers." Lord Derby was high-Victorian-, and Rieu mid-Windsor-steady.

Whatever these guides knew about the language in which the *Iliad* was composed they gave me a dissimilar impression of the work that had inspired their own, and this variety, plus regular *On Homer* tutorials from Carne-Ross, supported my plan to retain Homer's story line, to cut or amplify or add to its incidents, vary its similes, and (mostly) omit Homer's descriptive epithets: "ten-second-miler-Achilles," "never-defeated Ajax," and so forth.

As the work progressed I paid less attention to my guides. Carne-Ross provided translations retaining the Greek word order; I concocted a new story line; and then, knowing the gist of what this or that character said, tried to make their voices come alive and to keep the action on the move.

Rather than a translation in the accepted sense of the word, I was writing what I hoped would turn out to be a poem in English dependent upon whatever, through reading and through conversation,

I could guess about a small part of the *Iliad*, a poem whose composition is reckoned to have preceded the beginnings of our own written language by fifteen centuries.

My reading on the subject of translation had produced at least one important opinion: "We must try its effect as an English poem," Boswell reports Johnson as saying; "that is the way to judge of the merit of a translation."

I chose the passages which became *Patrocleia* and *Pax* on the advice of Carne-Ross. "Book 16, or *Patrocleia*," he said, "might be described as a miniature *Iliad*. It has a quarrel, a making-up, a concession, several battles, the death of a famous leader (Sarpedon), disagreement in Heaven, a human cheeking the gods, and, as a result of that human's death, irreversible change.

"In addition, *Patrocleia* contains the *Iliad*'s crucial twist: through the death of Patroclus, Achilles returns to the fight, thereby ensuring the destruction of Troy."

Pax is its opposite: disaffected allies settling their differences to avoid defeat at the hands of a mutual enemy. It exemplifies the public confession of common sins righted by material compensation and absolved by formal sacrifice.

With *Pax* completed, I realized that conflating Books 17 and 18 as *GBH* (Grievous Bodily Harm, an English legal term for serious forms of criminal assault) would allow me to try my hand at something new—600-odd lines devoted almost entirely to violent, mass action—which would unite *Patrocleia* and *Pax*.

After *Patrocleia* was published I began to get critical support not only from those connected with the composition and publication of verse but from those whom we may choose to count among the hopelessly insane: the hard core of Unprofessional Ancient Greek Readers, Homer's lay fans.

Welcome as the support of my like had been, as encouraging, and critically speaking more useful, were my contacts with such fans. "Quite good that bit of Homer you did," one might say. "If you do more of it, have a look at"—citing a favourite passage—"and in case you need any help with the words—take my card."

What I learned from those Homerniks clarified the guesses I made about the transmitted text, encouraging me to continue work on what I began to think of as "my Homer poem" with *Kings: An Account of Books 1 and 2 of Homer's "Iliad,"* and with *The Husbands: An Account of Books 3 and 4* of Homer's poem, these books because they form the poem's first movement (no warfare until Book 5) and because by this time I knew enough about the *Iliad* to see a way of using its material through to—well, as (among other things) Homer teaches you not to count your chickens, let me say no more than some of the *Iliad*'s later books.

Kings sets the poem up. I added the sacrifice (pages 32–36) and the scenes in Troy: the first to emphasize the immanence of religious feeling expressed by the poem, the second to establish Hector, and Troy, early on.

By title, *The Husbands* situates Helen, her predicament, her role, her rightlessness, at the centre of the piece; Paris and Menelaos are her adjuncts. As well, I wished to develop the contrast I find between her and Andromache.

If I can continue the poem the difference between these women will become clear.

Even though it owes its life to ridicule or to the power of bad taste, any poem that survives outside literary circles for more than one generation is noteworthy.

For a poem of over 15,000 lines representing an age as remote from its own as it is from ours to survive the collapse of, not just one society (a serious critical test no poem in English has, as yet, had to pass), but two, could easily mean that those who have kept it alive are mad.

And if it follows that those who read the *Iliad* in translation or recomposition are merely a bit touched, some of our problems become clearer: Pope earned the equivalent of £100,000 from his Homer work; my edition of Lord Derby's *Iliad* is its fifth; two million copies of Rieu's version have been sold. In fact, any deficiencies of length or of vigour you may find in what follows may be ascribed to my concern for public health.

For critical, and for financial, support while writing *War Music* I am much indebted: for the first, to the late Lindsay Anderson, Liane Aukin, the late Sally Belfrage, Charles Rowan Beye, James Campbell, Donald Carne-Ross, Jasper Griffin, Michael Hastings, Colin Leach, Peter Levi, Ruth Padel, George Plimpton, Bernard Pomerance, Craig Raine, Kathleen Raine, the late George Rapp, the late Stephen Spender, George Steiner, and to my editors in London and in New York, Christopher Reid and Aoibheann Sweeney; for the second, to Raymond Danowski, Bernard Pomerance, Bernard Stone, the Arts Council of Great Britain, the Bollingen Foundation (that was), the Drama (Radio) Department of the BBC, the Society of Authors, Transon Holdings, and Lord Weidenfeld. As well, I would like to thank Mme Jacques Brel, Hugo Claus, Ian Hamilton Finlay, Robert Fogarty, Alastair Fowler, John Gross, Shusha Guppy, Melville Hardiment, Christian Hesketh, Philip Howard, Oona Lahr, Andrew Motion, John Simpson of the Oxford University Press, Christian Smith, Martin Taylor of the Department of Printed Books, Imperial War Museum, Michael Taylor, and Kathleen Tynan, all of whom wrote to me or spoke to others on my behalf.

Introduction

Translators come and go, but it is given to few poets to bring Homer crashing into their time, like a giant trampling forests. In English, only three have done it—George Chapman, Alexander Pope, and Christopher Logue.

All three, as they say, "take liberties," but not to get away from Homer. Theirs are tremendous efforts *toward* him. Poets who cannot or will not take such risks never get near their man. They assemble dictionary equivalents, like that unoffending *prosateur* Richmond Lattimore, and call the result an epic.

Since Logue does not call his work a translation of Homer but an "account" of him, some think he is just offering his own Trojan story, as Chaucer or Shakespeare did in their Troilus poems. But Logue is striving to reach the essence of Homer, including those things hardest to bring over into our culture, the things most easily jettisoned if one is inventing a contemporary entertainment. Homer without theophanies, animal sacrifice, catalogues, epithets, or repeated speeches is not Homer. That is why Shakespeare's *Troilus and Cressida* is not Homer, or anything like Homer.

Animal sacrifice is pivotal to great events in the *Iliad*. The gods must be brought into the action, by ritual procedures foreign to us:

> First they drew back the victims' heads and
>   slaughtered them and skinned them,
> and cut away the meat from the thighs and
>   wrapped them in fat,
> making a double fold, and laid shreds of flesh upon
>   them.

Lattimore printed these lines as poetry and probably thought they were. They do have the relevant animal innards. But what sacrifice *meant* to Homer is nowhere to be found in Lattimore; his lines do no work in the poem—to avert plague, or protect men in battle. We are taken nowhere near that combination of charnel-house gore and out-of-time exaltation that Walter Burckardt or René Girard found for us in the act of sacrifice. We do not see how a bond is forged with the victim, who seems to collaborate in its own destruction, or how life spurts from death.

Logue can make his sacrifices *function* again:

> The heroes filled their drinking cups with wine
> Sainted with water, which is best, and sipped;
> And what in them was noble, grew;
> And truthfulness, with many meanings, spread
> Over the slopes and through the leafy spears
> As Priam thrust the knife into the white lamb's throat
> (Which did not struggle very much) and pressed it down,
> Into the black lamb's throat, and pressed it down;
> Then, as the overlords spilt out their cups,
> Lifted the pan of blood Talthibios had caught,
> Bright red in silver to the sun.

I leave even better sacrifice scenes for the reader to find, since they are too extended to be quoted in an introduction.

When the gods are not being called down by human acts, they break into the course of things with brutal willfulness. These theophanies offended Plato. There is a slapstick cruelty in such trivial use of tremendous power. Later pieties have softened the challenge of such divine captiousness. Even Chapman and Pope, those great poets, make Athena's intervention in Book 1 a symbolic checking of Achilles' passion with the voice of reason. But Athena grabs him by the hair and jerks him around. It is as if his father's ghost *tackled* Hamlet as he railed against Gertrude. Only Logue catches the weird interplay of god and human at that point.

Yet Logue conveys as well the sweet protectiveness that emanates from gods:

And Apollo took Sarpedon out of range
And clarified his wounds with mountain water;
Moistened his body with tinctures of white myrrh
And violet iodine; and when these chrisms dried
He folded him in miniver and lints
That never wear, that never fade,
And called God's two blind footmen, Sleep and Death,
Who carried him
Before whose memory the stones shall fade
To Lycia by Taurus.

That passage repeats almost verbatim two earlier speeches describing what Zeus desires—one of several ways Logue makes the repeated formulas of Homer work in a modern poem.

Aphrodite is another matter. There is high comedy in the way she has to bully Helen and Paris into pleasure. Paris pouts to Hector that Aphrodite *forces* him to be pretty (3.64–66). Helen sickens at the power of Aphrodite to make her desire again what she despises. Lattimore thinks the latter conflict is struck off in this primness: "Strange divinity! Why are you still so stubborn to beguile me?" (3.399). All of Homer's intricate comedy goes into Aphrodite's rescue of Paris from the battlefield. Since even human heroes can throw mountains in Homer, gods have to be more spectacular in their interference with natural law. Aphrodite, whose trait is laughter (5.375), whose trademark is beauty, can pluck up and out—*ex-erpaks(e)*—a big man, armor and all, wrap him in invisible airs, and settle him in a nest of perfumes (3.380–82). Logue, who uses only select parts of the *Iliad*, pours the whole of Aphrodite's subversive power into this theophany: she who turns the despised into the desired can turn swords into her attendant doves:

A hundred of us pitch our swords to him . . .
Yet even as they flew, their blades
Changed into wings, their pommels into heads,
Their hilts to feathered chests, and what were swords

Were turned to doves, a swirl of doves,
And waltzing out of it, in oyster silk,
Running her tongue around her strawberry lips
While repositioning a spaghetti shoulder-strap,
The Queen of Love, Our Lady Aphrodite,
Touching the massive Greek aside with one
Pink fingertip, and with her other hand
Lifting Lord Paris up, big as he was,
In his bronze bodice heavy as he was,
Lacing his fingers with her own, then leading him,
Hidden in wings, away.

Some critics have been shocked by that passage; but Plato knew that we *should* be shocked by Homer's gods. It has been asked, in particular, where the "spaghetti shoulder-strap" comes from. Well, Aphrodite's supreme aphrodisiac is the "embroidered thong" (*kestos himas*, 14.214) Hera borrows from her—which is either a "cincture" to nip in the chiton under her breast, or a crisscross strap at the cleavage which the most authoritative recent commentary on the *Iliad* calls a "sexy brassiere" (Janko, 1992, in the G. S. Kirk series). Aphrodite's identification with sex-triggering dress is clearly Homeric.

Despite such authentically Homeric hijinks, no one can suggest with more economy than Logue the numinous quality of divine action—as when Achilles takes up the weird armor made for him in Heaven:

And as she laid the moonlit armour on the sand
It chimed . . .
  [Achilles] looked,
Lifted a piece of it between his hands;
Turned it; tested the weight of it; and then
Spun the holy tungsten like a star between his knees . . .

The famous catalogue of forces in Book 2 Logue turns into a stream of weapons and troops and banners, all funneling toward war, with repetitions of the word "bronze" like a great gong struck over and over—an effect he borrows from Eliot's *Coriolan*.

Logue also understands the magic of Homer's similes—that they work by a process of inverse suggestion: peaceful acts compared with war create a sense of things chiming from opposite poles.

> Try to recall the pause, thock, pause,
> Made by axe blades as they pace
> Each other through a valuable wood.
> Though the work takes place on the far
> Side of a valley, and the axe strokes are
> Muted by depths of warm, still standing, air,
> They throb, throb, closely in your ear;
> And now and then you catch a phrase
> Exchanged between the men who work
> More than a mile away, with perfect clarity.
>
> Likewise the sound of spear on spear,
> Shield against shield, shield against spear
> Around Sarpedon's body.

Here as elsewhere, Logue has taken a hint from Chapman (one of many poets put to new uses in Logue's poem):

> And then, as in sounding vale (near neighbour to a hill)
> Wood-fellers make a far-heard noise, with chopping,
>   chopping still . . .
> (Iliad 16.586–87)

One escapes the din and immediacy of the scene around Sarpedon's body to see the blows, as it were, in slow motion—the effect Kurosawa achieves when a battle is slowed, its sound suppressed, the dreamlike delirium of battle made more real by a muting and containing of its horror. Nietzsche described this effect as the recruiting of Apollo to capture a vision that Dionysus would dissolve in rending ecstasy. The similes give Apolline control to Dionysiac action. What could be more mundane than fishing—unless it be eating fish from a tin? Homer uses homely bits of daily life, however distantly fetched, to steady the horror of his battle scenes. Logue recruits as broadly as Homer, who gave us all of *his* known world:

> They passed so close that hub skinned hub.
> Ahead, Patroclus braked a shade, and then,
> And gracefully as men in oilskins cast
> Fake insects over trout, he speared the boy,
> And with his hip his pivot, prised Thestor up and out
> As easily as later men detach
> A sardine from an opened tin.

That shift from one simile to another—fishing from water, then fishing from a tin—is also typical of Homer.

One reason for the magic distancing achieved by Homeric similes is that the main action is remembered from a heroic past while the similes draw on the daily life of Homer's contemporaries. Milton understood that, and used a Homeric simile to link the cosmology of the Bible with the most advanced scientific work of his own day. In *Paradise Lost* (1.287–91), Satan bears a shield

> Hung on his shoulders like the moon, whose orb
> Through optic glass the Tuscan artist [Galileo] views
> At evening from the top of Fesole,
> Or in Valdarno, to descry new lands,
> Rivers or mountains in her spotty globe.

In the same way, Logue makes the talking horses of Achilles seem at home with the miraculous when he refers to the magic carriages of modern science:

> The chariot's basket dips. The whip
> Fires in between the horses' ears.

And as in dreams, or at Cape Kennedy, they rise,
Slowly it seems, their chests like royals, yet
Behind them in a double plume the sand curls up,
Is barely dented by their flying hooves,
And wheels that barely touch the world,
And the wind slams shut behind them.

Logue's inclusiveness is the marvel. He gets the drive and almost frenzied energy of Chapman. Yet he can achieve the epigrammatic and rhetorical poise of Pope—he gives a classical feel to his verse by balanced constructions like this:

Touching his welts with *one*
And with the knuckles of his *other* hand
Wiping his tears away. [Italics added.]

Logue has all of Simone Weil's disgust for war. But Weil could not admit the fierce joy in battle, which means that much of Homer was a closed book to her. Logue sees injustice and valor, reality and transcendence, all dancing warily about one another. In Homer's world, the familiar and the strange look at each other in mutual incomprehension and respect. This leads to Logue's most daring step, the treatment of Troy as a third-world country, to suggest colonial warfare. His warrant is the exotic and fairy-tale quality of Priam's rule—his harem and his fifty sons (only nineteen of them Hecuba's —see 24.496). The sense of two different cultures clashing is emphasized in the first engagement of troops in the epic, where Trojan babble is the mark of *barbaroi*:

Think of the noise that fills the air
When autumn takes the Dnepr by the arm
And skein on skein of honking geese fly south
To give the stateless rains a miss:
So Hector's moon-horned, shouting dukes
Burst from the tunnels, down the slope,

And shout, shout, shout, smashed shouted shout
Backward and forth across the sky;
While pace on pace the Greeks came down the counterslope
With blank, unyielding imperturbability.

It is true that the Trojans speak Greek, to others and themselves, but what else could they speak? In our World War II movies, Germans are clearly speaking German when alone with one another, but we hear it as English. The Trojans twittering like cicadas around Priam on his Wall hint at differences that cannot be spelled out any further. The Trojans have the same gods as the Greeks—but barbarians were expected to. Besides, the two sides have different *patrons* on Olympus. We cannot expect our own anthropological awareness of societal differences from Homer, but there are constant hints that Homer thought of Trojan life as different from the Hellenic. Logue follows the logic of those indications.

This emphasis on cultural separations just brings home more powerfully the deepest insight Logue has into Homer: that over and over men literally kill *themselves* in battle. Achilles kills Achilles when he slays Hector, since Hector is wearing the armor Achilles gave to Patroclus, willing him his own identity. The dying Patroclus says he hears death call his name—and it is "Hector." The men's fates are all reversible-identical. When Hector takes up the dangerous beauty of Achilles' armor, he is at first elated, lifted up to his adversary's level. His limbs magically fill out any looseness in the harness. But he is stepping, literally, outside his own limits, losing himself in the larger meshes of Achilles' doom. In becoming "more than himself," he says goodbye to his proper world, reflected in the armor as a glimpse of pastoral (a kind of visual simile). Logue has borrowed, here, the scenes Achilles studies on his *second* shield; but that only emphasizes the two men's interconnectedness of fates:

Achilles' armour was not made on earth.
The lame god yoked its spacious particles.
Deliberate inattention has

Only enhanced its light-collecting planes;
Into whose depth, safe, safe, amid the dunes
Prince Hector looks, amazed, and strips his own;
Stands naked in the light, amazed, and lifts
Its bodice up, and kisses it; then holds it out,
And, like a man long kept from water, lets
Its radiance pour down; and sees within
The clouds that pass, the gulls that stall,
His own hope-governed face, and near its rim,
Distorted as the brilliant surface bends
Its rivetless, near-minus weight away,
His patient horses, and his men.

Great poetry. But is it Homer? Yes—all the way down, in deepening gyres, to the *Iliad*'s inmost core.

—Garry Wills

Kings

1

Picture the east Aegean sea by night,
And on a beach aslant its shimmering
Upwards of 50,000 men
Asleep like spoons beside their lethal Fleet.

  Now look along that beach, and see
Between the keels hatching its western dunes
A ten-foot-high reed wall faced with black clay
And split by a double-doored gate;
Then through the gate a naked man
Whose beauty's silent power stops your heart
Fast walk, face wet with tears, out past its guard,
And having vanished from their sight
Run with what seems to break the speed of light
Across the dry, then damp, then sand invisible
Beneath inch-high waves that slide
Over each other's luminescent panes;
Then kneel among those panes, beggar his arms, and say:

  "Source, hear my voice.
God is your friend. You had me to serve Him.
In turn, He swore: If I, your only child,
Chose to die young, by violence, far from home,
My standing would be first; be best;   ⌉ critical?
The best of bests; here; and in perpetuity. ⌋
  And so I chose. Nor have I changed. But now—
By which I mean today, this instant, now—
That Shepherd of the Clouds has seen me trashed
Surely as if He sent a hand to shoo

5

The army into one, and then, before its eyes,
Painted my body with fresh Trojan excrement."

    Sometimes
Before the gods appear
Something is marked:
    A noise. A note, perhaps. Perhaps
A change of temperature. Or else, as now,
The scent of oceanic lavender,
That even as it drew his mind
Drew from the seal-coloured sea onto the beach
A mist that moved like weed, then stood, then turned
Into his mother, Thetis', mother lovelost face,
Her fingers, next, that lift his chin, that push
His long, redcurrant-coloured hair
Back from his face, her voice, her words:

    "Why tears, Achilles?
Rest in my arms and answer from your heart."

    The sea as quiet as light.

    "Three weeks ago," he said, "while raiding southern Ilium
I killed the men and stripped a town called Tollo
Whose yield comprised a wing of Hittite chariots
And 30 fertile women.
    As is required
The latter reached the beach-head unassigned,
Were sorted by the herald's staff, and then
Soon after sunrise on the following day
Led to the common sand for distribution.
    At which point, mother mine"—his tears have gone—
"Enter the King. No-no. Our King of kings, Majestic Agamemnon,
His nose extruded from his lionshead cowl,
Its silvered claws clasped so"—arms over chest—

"And sloping up his shoulder, thus, the mace,
The solar mace, that stands for—so I thought—
What Greeks require of Greeks:
   To worship God; to cherish honour;
To fight courageously, keeping your own,
And so the status of your fellow lords
High, mother, high—as he knows well—as he knew well—
As he came walking through those culled
By acclamation when the best
Meet for herald Stentor's 'Who is owed?'
To view the 30 captive shes—
Among them six with infant boys at heel—
Here sniffing, pinching here, lifting a lip, a lid,
Asking his brother: 'One, Menelaos, or . . . or two?'
   Then having scanned their anxious faces with his own
The guardian of our people outs the mace
As if it was a mop, and with its gold
Egg-ended butt, selects—before the owed—
A gently broken adolescent she
Who came—it seemed—from plain but prosperous ground."

   "First King, first fruit," his mother said.
"Will you hear more, or not?" he said.
"Dear child . . ."
"Then do not interrupt."

   The stars look down.
Troy is a glow behind the dunes.
The camp is dark.

   "Her name was Cryzia," Achilles said.
"Less than a week
After she went through Agamemnon's gate,
Her father, Cryzez of Cape Tollomon,
The archpriest of Apollo's coastal sanctuary,

7

Came to the beach-head, up, between the ships,
Holding before him, outright, with both hands
An ivory rod adorned with streams of wool,
Twice consecrated to that Lord of Light.
    Pausing an instant by Odysseus' ship—
Our centrepoint—
He reached the middle of the common sand, and,
With the red fillets blowing round his shaven head,
Waited until its banks were packed.
Then offered all, but principally
King Agamemnon and his queenless brother,
Two shipholds of amphorae filled with Lycian wine,
A fleet of Turkey mules,
2,000 sheepskins, cured, cut, and sewn,
To have his daughter back: plus these gloved words:

    'Paramount Agamemnon, King of kings,
The Lord of Mainland and of Island Greece,
May God Almighty grant that you,
And those who follow you,
Demolish Troy, then sail safe home.
    Only take these commodities for my child,
So tendering your mercy to God's son,
Apollo, Lord of Light and Mice.'

    'Yes!'
    'Yes!'
    'Yes!'
    'Yes!'

    "The fighters cried,
And Yes to them—but to themselves—the lords.

    "You would have thought the matter done.
A bargain; with himself—

8

Well over 40 if a day—
Having had, and then released, a dozen such
For general use.
    But no.
Before the fourth Yes died our guardian Lord began:

    'As my pronouncement will affect you all,
Restrain your Yessings,' yes, and when we did,
    'If,' he continues, 'if, priest, if
When I complete the things I am about to say,
I catch you loitering around our Fleet
Ever again, I shall, with you in one,
And in my other hand your mumbo rod,
Thrash you until your eyeballs shoot.
    As for your child:
Bearing by night my body in my bed,
Bearing by day my children on her knee,
Soft in the depths of my ancestral house,
If ever she sees Ilium again
She will have empty gums.
    Be safe—begone. For good.'

    "Fearful as the toad in a python's mouth,
The priest, as if the world was empty, walked away
Beside the sea, then hung his head and prayed
Wet-cassocked in the foam:

    'Mousegod,
    Whose reach makes distance myth,
    In whose abundant warmth
    The vocal headlands of Cape Tollomon bask,
    As all my life I dressed your leafy shrine
    And have, with daily holocausts,
    Honoured your timeless might,
    Vouchsafe me this:

9

For every hair upon my daughter's head
Let three Greeks die.'"

Barely a pace
Above the Mediterranean's sandy edge,
Mother and child.
     And as she asks: "Then what?"
Their early pietà dissolves,
And we move ten days back.

Long after midnight when you park, and stand
Just for a moment in the chromium wash,
Sometimes it seems that, some way off,
Between the river and the tower belt, say,
The roofs show black on pomegranate red
As if, below that line, they stood on fire.

Lights similar to these were seen
By those who looked from Troy towards the Fleet
After Apollo answered Cryzez' prayer.

Taking a corner of the sky
Between his finger and his thumb,
Out of its blue, as boys do towels, he cracked
Then zephyr-ferried in among the hulls
A generation of infected mice.

Such fleas . . .
Such lumps . . .
Watch Greece begin to die:

Busy in his delirium, see Tek
(A carpenter from Mykonos) as he comes forward, hit—

10

It seems—by a stray stone, yet still comes on,
Though coming now as if he walked a plank,
Then falling off it into nothingness.
   See 30—dead in file,
Their budded tongues crystallized with green fur,
As daily to the fire-pits more cart more,
As half, it seemed, incinerated half,
And sucking on their masks
The cremators polluted Heaven.

   "Home . . ."
   "Home . . ."

   Nine days.
And on the next, Ajax,
Grim underneath his tan as Rommel after 'Alamein,
Summoned the army to the common sand,
Raised his five-acre voice, and said:

   "Fighters!
Hear what my head is saying to my heart:
   Have we forgotten to say our prayers?
One thing is sure: the Trojans, or the mice,
Will finish us unless God helps.
   We are not short of those who see beyond the facts.
Let them advise. High smoke can make amends."

   He sits.
Our quietude assents.
Ajax is loved. I mean it. He is *loved*.
Not just for physical magnificence
(The eyelets on his mesh like runway lights)
But this: no Greek—including Thetis' son—
Contains a heart so brave, so resolute, so true,
As this gigantic lord from Salamis.

The silence thickens.
Eyes slide, then slide away, then slide again
Onto the army's eldest augur, Calchas, who
Half rose, and having said:

"The Lord of Light finds Greece abominable,"

Half sat, sat, looked about, shirked Agamemnon's eye,
Caught ten as lordly, re-arose, and said:

"Kings lose their heads, but not their memories.
Who will protect me if I say
What Agamemnon does not want said?"

"Me,"

Said Achilles,
As he stood, lifted his palms, and swore:

"This before God:
From Ethiopia to Thrace,
From Babylon to the Hesperides,
As high—as low—as Idan peaks, or the Aegean's floor,
While I am still alive and killing, no one shall touch
You, sir, or anybody here who can say why
The Lord of Light finds Greece abominable—
And, sir, no one enlists our self-appointed first,
Best king, Lord Agamemnon of Mycenae."

Then sat beside his friend, his next, his heart,
Patroclus, lord Menotion's son,
While Calchas said (with sympathy for all):

"The sacred vermin came because,
Though offered more than due,

King Agamemnon would not give Apollo's priest
His soft-topped-eyed and squashed-mouth daughter back.
  Nor will they boil away
Until Lord Agamemnon, dueless now,
Resigns that daughter to her father's stock
With these winged words:
  Resume your child in Heaven's name,
And may the high smoke from the sacrifice
Of these 400 sheep
Propitiate the Lord of Mice and Light."

  Low ceiling. Sticky air.
Many draw breath
As Agamemnon, red with rage, yells:

[handwritten:] Sets a good scene]

  "Blindmouth!
Good words would rot your tongue."
  Then reads the warning in his brother's face
And says (half to himself):
  "Well, well, well, well . . .
You know your way around belief."
  Then looking out:
  "Greece knows I want this girl
More than I want the father-given, free-born she
Who rules Mycenae in my place—Greek Clytemnestra.
Although, unlike that queen, the girl has not
Parted a boy to bear my honoured name,
Yet as she stitches, stands, and speaks as well,
Raised to the rank of wife, so might she suckle."

The army breathes again.

  "However,
As being first means being privileged,

So privilege incurs responsibility.
And my responsibility is plain:
To keep the army whole. To see it hale.
To lead it through Troy's Skean Gate."

Again.

"Therefore,
With the addition of a Cretan bull,
To our religious entertainer's charge,
The girl, who brought me happiness,
Shall be returned to Tollomon."

Applause.

The lord of Crete, Idomeneo, starts to slip away.

"But . . ."

Then stops.

". . . as the loss of an allotted she
Diminishes my honour and my state,
Before the army leaves the common sand
Its captain lords will find among their own
Another such for me."

Low ceiling. Sticky air.
Our stillness like the stillness
In Atlantis as the big wave came,
The brim-full basins of abandoned docks,
Or Christmas morning by the sea.

Until Achilles said:

14

"Dear sir,
Where shall we get this she?
There is no pool.
We land. We fight. We kill. We load. And then—
After your firstlings—we allot.
That is the end of it.
We do not ask things back. And even you
Would not permit your helmet to go round.
    Leave her to Heaven.
And when—and if—God lets me leap the Wall
Greece will restock your dormitory."

    "Boy Achilleus," Agamemnon said,
"You will need better words
And more than much more charm
Before your theorizing lightens me.
    Myself unshe'd, and yours still smiling in the furs?
Ditchmud."

Ach is hypocritical.

    And widening his stare:
    "Consult. Produce a string. Cryzia was fit
To be covered by a god. So pick your tenderest. Or—
Now listen carefully—I shall be at your gate
Demanding Uxa, Ajax, or
At my lord Diomed's for Gwi,
Or leaving yours, truth's-pet, Achilles-san,
With Miss Briseis on my arm.
Kah!—What does it matter whose prize she I take?
But take I shall, and if needs be, by force.

    "Well . . .
We shall see.

    "And now
Let us select and stow a ship,

15

Captained by you, lord Thoal, or by you,
Our silencer, Idomeneo.
At all events, some diplomatic lord
To take my pretty Cryzia home
That holy smoke and thermal prayers
Commend the Son of God
To exorcize the insects we refresh."

"Amen . . ."

Then would have stood and gone, except
Achilles strode towards him, one arm up,
Jabbing his fist into the sky, and called:
    "Mouth! King mouth!"
Then stopped. Then from the middle of the common sand said:

    "Heroes, behold your King—
Slow as an arrow fired feathers first
To puff another's worth,
But watchful as a cockroach of his own.
    Behold his cause—
Me first, me second,
And if by chance there is a little left—me third.
    Behold his deeds—
Fair ransom scanted, and its donor spurned.
The upshot—plague.
    O Agamemnon, O King Great I Am,
The Greeks who follow you, who speak for you,
Who stand among the blades for you,
Prostitute loyalty.
    To me, the Ilians are innocent.
They have not fleeced my father's countryside.
Cloud-shadowing mountains and abyssal seas
Separate them from Pythia. And half the time
You Mycenean/Trojans seem to me

16

Like two bald men fighting over a comb.
　　If steal is right, my King,
It was a Spartan, not a Pythic wife
Cock Paris lifted from your brother's bed;
Your hospitality that platinum maggot slimed;
Your name, not mine, he sacked; and yours, not mine,
The battles I have sited, fought, and won.
　　'Well . . . We shall see.' Indeed.
Zero to zero. Dead cells. Shredded. Gone."

"True."
"True."

　　"Since I arrived, my Lord,
I have sent 20 lesser Ilian towns
Backwards into the smoke.
But when—as is required—we distribute,
To you the delicates, to me the dottle of their loss—
Except for her, Briseis, my ribbon she,
Whose fearless husband plus some 60
Handsome-bodied warriors I killed and burned
At Thebé-under-Ida as it burned,
And so was named her owner by your lords
In recognition of my strength, my courage, my superiority—
Although you will not treat me with respect.

　　"Well then, my Lord,
You change the terms, I change the tense.
　　Let is be was. Was to the day on which
Backlit by long-necked flames
You lead your Greeks necklaced with spoil
Capering along the road that tops the Wall.
Because you cannot take the city without me.
Pe'leus' son.
Because tomorrow I sail home."

Silence.

Reverse the shot.

Go close.

Hear Agamemnon, Lord of lords, Autarch of Argos,
Whose eminent domain includes all southern Greece:

"Many will say
Good riddance to bad rubbish.
I shall not.
　I am your King.
God called. God raised. God recognized.
　Nestor, Odysseus, Ajax,
Cretan Idomeneo, Diomed,
Thoal of Macedon, Jica of Thessaly,
Stand at my name.
　Look at them, boy. They are not muck.
They have been here nine years.
When you were what—a bubble on a dam?
Likewise the thousands in whose sight we stand.
They honour me. And I am popular.
　God made you fast. Some say the fastest. And some say
More beautiful than any other man.
Indubitably He made you strong and brave.
　So tell me this: who made you sour?
For you are sour, boy Achilleus, sour.
　Go home. Go now.
The time has come for you to see
More of your family.
And I am confident that he will find—
And we shall hear that he has found—
More honour in the cuckoo woods of Pythia
Than he has won at Troy."

Then to them all:
"Here is the news.
Before world-class Achilles sails,
As God has taken Cryzia from me
I shall take his best she, Briseis, from him.
   More.
Her confiscation shows, once and for all,
My absolute superiority,
Not just to you, retiring boy, but anyone
Stupid enough to challenge me
In word or deed."

   Achilles' face
Is like a chalkpit fringed with roaring wheat.
His brain says: "Kill him. Let the Greeks sail home."
His thigh steels flex.

   And then,
Much like a match-flame struck in full sunlight,
We lose him in the prussic glare
Teenage Athena, called the Daughter Prince—who burst
Howling and huge out of God's head—sheds
From her hard, wide-apart eyes, as she enters
And stops time.

   But those still dying see:
   Achilles leap the 15 yards between
Himself and Agamemnon;
Achilles land, and straighten up, in one;
Achilles' fingertips—such elegance!—
Push push-push push, push Agamemnon's chest;
The King lean back; Achilles grab
And twist the mace out of his royal hand
And lift it . . . Oh . . . flash! flash!
The heralds running up . . .

But we stay calm,
For we have seen Athena's radiant hand
Collar Achilles' plait,
Then as a child its favourite doll
Draw his head back towards her lips
To say:

"You know my voice?
You know my power?

"Be still.

"God's wife has sent me:
'Stop him. I like them both,' she said.
    I share her view.
If you can stick to speech, harass him now.
But try to kill him, and I kill you."

She goes,
And time restarts.

The mace.
King Agamemnon outs his hand.

Achilles says:

"I hate your voice, claw King. I hate its tune.
Lord of All Voices is God's fairest name.
Your voice defiles that name. Cuntstruck Agamemnon!
The King who would use force against his lord.
    O cheesey Lung,
I know as much, in likelihood much more,
About the use of force as any here,
Master or muster, first or flock, hero or herd,
And in my backwoods way have half a mind

To knock you multinational flat with this"—
His hand—"then bar your throat with this"—his foot—
"Kingman who never yet led star or store
Into the blades, or kept them there,
Or raised his blade alone—for no one doubts,
Hector, the light of Priam's 50 sons,
Would, if you raised it, see your arm.

   Kih! I forgot. Our King is philosophical;
He fears his youth has gone; he will not fight, today.
Tomorrow, then? Tomorrow we will see.
Indeed, boy Achilleus—as my dear father says—
Boy Achilleus, you are wrong to criticize.
Atreus is King. What need has he to keep
A helicopter whumphing in the dunes,
Being popular, with his commanders at his heel?
Who will not stand to speak to me."

   "Shame . . ."

   "Captains,
I was too young to take the oath you swore
When Helen's father said:
   'This womb is now a wife,'
And handed her to you, brave Menelaos.
But each to each vowed in the name of God:

   'If she, our loveliest, is stolen, or she strays,
As we are all her husbands,
Each of us, heedless of cost,
Will be in honour bound to bring her back.'

   "So here you are.

   "Shame that your King is not so bound to you
As he is bound to what he sniffs. And bound to mute

21

The voice that hints, just hints, he might be, um . . .
Not wrong, of course, ah . . . how shall we put it?—
A hair's-breadth less than absolutely right.

   "Here is the truth:
King Agamemnon is not honour bound.
Honour to Agamemnon is a thing
That he can pick, pick up, put back, pick up again,
A somesuch you might find beneath your bed.
   Do not tell Agamemnon honour is
No mortal thing, but ever in creation,
Vital, free, like speed, like light,
Like silence, like the gods,
The movement of the stars! Beyond the stars!
Dividing man from beast, hero from host,
That proves best, best, that only death can reach,
Yet cannot die because it will be said, be sung,
Now, and in time to be, for evermore."

   "Amen."
   "He is so beautiful."
   "Without him we are lost."
Thoal, then Menelaos, then Odysseus said
(But only to themselves) as he swept on:

   "I do not fear you, King. Your voice is false,"
Then lifts his arm and makes a T—
   "You tax where you should tender, feed where fend"—
Out of its upright with the mace as bar.
   "This mace objectifies custom and truth.
Hephaestus, the Lame Lord of Fire,
Made it to glorify our Father, God,
When cosmos conquered chaos at His touch.
Mortals who tote it are required to bring

Fair judgement out of Heaven to earth.
   By it, hear this:
Call at our gate, King; my Patroclus will
Surrender Briseis. Touch else of ours,
And I will snap your back across my knee.
   But from now on,
Seeing your leadership has left me leaderless,
I shall not fight for you, or by your side,
Or for, or by, these federal lords that let you live.
   Those who believe that I am in the right,
Speak now: or never speak to me again."

No sound.

Lord Thoal thinks: "Boy, boy,
You have not heard a word he said,
And in a moment you will say
Our silence has betrayed you."

Still no sound.

A whinny. Wings. The wheezing of the sea.
And so he dropped the mace.

   Then
   Drinking his tears
Achilles called into the sky:

   "Which will you see, great clouds?
Troy's topless towers fall to his voice,
Or Greece to pieces in his hands?"
   And wiping them away:
   "You lords will be his widows. Tiger bait.
Down plain, or in the dunes there, kih!—

Troy has come. Aeneas and Prince Paris come,
Moved on your Fleet by music, trumpets come,
In one wide cry of rage, Sarpedon come.
The sea will ring with it. The sea will clap its hands.
And Hector, yes, his shout alone will burst you wide.
Then neither ditch, ramp, main camp track,
Nor double row of ships that drape the bay
Headland to headland will protect your knees
As you run down the beach.
   Please do not say
'If this comes true, Achilles will relent.'
Witness me glad. Yes. Glad. Extra glad when
Longing for me makes every one of you
Reach in his own broad chest,
Take out, and suck, his heart,
Then spit its extract in his neighbour's face,
Ashamed, that you, the Greek commander lords,
Dishonoured and betrayed boy Achilleus,
Promised by God, the best of the Acheans."

The world is shut.

   Talthibios, chief herald of the Greeks,
Nods to a lesser indeterminate
Who lifts, then takes, the mace to Agamemnon,
Still sitting on his stool.
Then bow-backs out before that King concludes:

   "Thank you, Greece.
As is so often true,
Silence has won the argument.
Achilles speaks as if I found you on a vase.
So leave his stone-age values to the sky."

24

A few loose claps,
And those around the army's voice,
Thersites of Euboea, say
(Not all that loudly):

"I told you so."
"Shame . . ."
"Home . . ."

Silence again.

And as Achilles strode away without a word,
Without a word Patroclus followed him.

Low on the hillsides to the east of Troy,
Women, waist-deep in dusk, shoulder their baskets
And, ascending, see the Wall's dark edge
Level the slopes it covers; and above,
Riding a lake of tiles,
The Temple on the sunset-lit Acropolis
Whose columns stripe the arrowhead
The rivers Sy'mois and Scamander make
As they meet, whose point flows out, flows on, until,
Imagined more than seen,
King Agamemnon's army stands
(As in the sepias of Gallipoli)
Thigh-deep, chest-deep,
Out from the spits where buffalo graze,
Heaping the ocean's ember blue
Over their curls, over their shoulders, as they pray:

"Dear Lord of Light, reclaim your mice,"

ough their faces, oars aloft,
a wreathed beneath its scorpion tail,
bull:

ear Lord of Light,"

High smoke behind them, Hesperus above,
The tribute ship is handed south.

Moist wind. Black wind. Rainbearing wind.
The tents like lanterns; green beneath dark hulls.
    Walking between them, lower lip upthrust,
The corners of his mouth pulled down, Nestor,
The lord of Sandy Pylos, cloaked and calm,
Past 80 if a day:
    "To see,"
Accompanied by his son, Antilochos,
    "Achilles."

Nod.
Look.
The gate.
The compound.
Then:
Achilles' tent, a moonlit, Cubist, dune.

Redcurrant hair seats white.

Dark wine in gold.

A sip.

"Shame on you both.

26

And more on you than him.
    I did not come this far to hear
That Troy is innocent.
    Troy is not innocent.
    Troy lies.
    Troy steals.
    Troy harbours thieves.

    "You are the same age as my son.
He worships you. Ask him,
That boy will follow you through arrowfire like rain.
My sticks are cut.
It is my place to tell you right from wrong.
    Far better men than you have seen the sky
And I have fought beside, and saved, their like;
And I have fought against, and killed, their like;
And when the fight was done I let
Those still standing know how victors act:
And they obeyed me.
    You are a child in parliament.
Someone talks common-nonsense and—tarrah!—
You give his words a future. Let them die.
You swear; and you are sworn. The world must change.
Speak to the gods if you want change.
    Great people promise more than they perform,
And you expect too much from promising.
    Be still!
Do not tell me Lord Agamemnon has enough.
I know Lord Agamemnon has enough.
But that is how Lord Agamemnon is.
Requiring. It is his due.
    The mace was left to him.
He lords more men, more land, more sea
Than any other Greek.
You are part dust, part deity.

But he is King. And so, for Greece, comes first.
   Honour his rank, honour your name.
But as Thersites' eczema words
Put off our taking Troy by putting 'Home!' 'Home!'
Into the army's mind, your 'Home' eggs his—
And all the other gash that tumbles out
Of his sisal-ball head.
   Thersites of Euboea, blustering rat;
Pe'leus' son, Achilles;
To link them in a sentence is to lie."

Their shadows on the textile.

"Think of the day when I and Ajax drove
Out of the trees towards Pe'leus' house
And waited in its gateway while he poured
Bright wine along the thigh-cuts off a steer
Just sacrificed to God—Guardian of Kings,
The Lord of Guests—when you,
Noticing us and springing up in one,
Ran to the gateway, took our hands, and led us in.
Kind boy. Good boy . . . And then,
When all had had enough to eat and drink,
Big Ajax asked if you and your dear heart,
Patroclus, could join the Greeks at Troy,
And he said yes. Then eyed you up and down,
And told you: One: to be the best.
To stand among the blades where honour grows,
Where fame is won, untouched by fear,
Counting on Hera and Athene for your strength—
If they so will. And Two: to mind your tongue."

   "He also said," Achilles said,
"That lordship knows the difference between

Anger and outrage. That the first
Is cured by time, or by revenge,
But outrage has a claim beyond itself.
    That not being so, why are we here, dear father friend?"

Gold holly in the hearth.

"Boy," Nestor said, "you are my soul.
Spirit, and strength, and beauty have combined
Such awesome power in you
A vacant Heaven would offer you its throne.
    If I, your grounded honourer,
Persuade the King and his confederates to leave
Briseis still your she, and no more said,
Will you be as you were—our edge?
    Look in my eyes, and answer."

Host.

Guest.

Patroclus—his face kept down.

Firelight against a painted box.

10,000 miles away
A giant child rests her chin on the horizon
And blows a city down.

Then a new voice:

"Father."
"I ordered you to wait."
"The King has sent Talthibios for Briseis."

The lamps lap oil.

"Fetch her, Patroclus," Achilles said.
And then:
"Time-honoured lord of Pylos,
Your voice is honey and your words are winged.
I hope we meet again."

His awning. At its edge

Talthibios and Kartom on their knees.

Taking their elbows. Raising them.

"Do not embarrass me.
I know that you have no share in the blame."

They stand. But back—
As most men do when facing him.

"Patroclus will bring her.
Tell the commanders who may ask I meant my words.
    I hate their King. He is a needle in my bread.
He is water. I am air. I honour you. Go.
Go."

And when he was alone he soiled himself,
His body and his face, with ash.
Then, naked, walked, half walked, half trotted out,
Face wet with tears, across his court,
Now past its gate, its guard,
And, having vanished from their sight,
Ran fast enough to overtake the light
To call his mother from the sea:
As we have seen.

Observe their walk. The goddess, Thetis, small
And sadly sensual, turning her lavish face
Upsideways to her frightening son,
Whose ash-streaked arm arches her shoulders, down her side,
Who says, and says, and says:

"That is the whole of it.
The Greeks have let their King take my prize she.
And now they aim to privatize that wrong,
Make it Achilles' brain-ache, fireside, thing.
   So go to God.
Press Him. Yourself against Him. Kiss His knees.
Say it again: 'Because I knew our son would take Your life,
I shut myself; and You
Gave me to lord Pe'leus out of pique.'
   Then beg Him this:
Till they come running to your actual son,
Let the Greeks burn, let them taste pain,
Asphyxiate their hope, so as their blood soaks down into the sand
Or as they sink like coins into the sea,
They learn."

"I love you, child. But we are caught.
You will die soon. As promised. And alone.
While I shall live for ever with my tears.
Keep your hate warm. God will agree," his mother said,

   And walked into the waves,
As he went up the beach towards his ship,
Towards the two great armies, all asleep.

Water, white water, blue-black here, without—
Past a turtle asleep on the sea—

Our animals hearing those closest ashore.
    Swell-water, black-water—
The breeze in the cliff pines, their hairpins, their resin,
And—
As we glide through their cleft—
Sheep bells greet ship's bell—
And the sea is

Suddenly, warm sky-blue as the light
Dives and returns from the sandy floor
As we lower, lose way, set oars, and regain it—
Then stroke the wide still ring
Of Cape Tollomon's echoing bay—
At our peak (now we ship them)
Lord Thoal's hand on her shoulder—
Cryzia, her eyes in her father's, and him—
With many (his choir, his dancers) "Sing Ave!"—
His eyes in his daughter's—"Sing Ave!"—and then,
As Thoal hands her ashore:
    "Sing Ave!"
    "Sing Ave!"
Once more in his arms.

    And when that solemn time had passed:

    "Priest of Apollo's coastal sanctuary,"
Lord Thoal said,
"The Lord of Mainland and of Island Greece,
Paramount Agamemnon, my true King,
Bid me to lead your child into your arms.
    Thereafterwards,
That their high smoke, and our encircling prayers
Appease the one whose vermin Greece infects,
Joint-voiced, we sacrifice these lovely animals

To God's first son, Apollo born,
The Lord of Light and Mice."

   The altar is oval, made of red quartz,
And broad-leaved plane trees shade the turf it crowns.
   Hear them come!
"Let the Greeks bring the knife"
   Here they come!
By the stream that freshens the bearded grass
   "To slit the bull's throat"
Wading the orchids that verge the turf
   "And we will carry the bowls
Of mountain water and sainted wine,
And the axe."
   "Pae'an!"
   Hear their song!
As their pale feet darken the fragrant turf:
   "Pae'an!" ——→ War Cry

They have come.

See the bull at the stone
"Lord of Light!"
See its gilded horns
"Lord of Light!"
See the axe.

Now the lustral water is on their hands,
And the barley sprinkled on the bull's wide head.
   "Bring the axe."
   "Pae'an!"
   "Lord of Mice!"

"Lord of Light! Light! Light!"
As the axe swings up, and stays,
　　"Pae'an!"
Stays poised, still poised, and—
As it comes down:
　　"PLEASE GOD!"
　　"PLEASE GOD!" *Who says this?*
Covers the terrible thock that parts the bull from its voice

　　"Pae'an!" → *Ritual, repetition*

As the knife goes in, goes down
And the dewlap parts like glue
And the great thing kneels
And its breath hoses out
And the authorized butchers grope for its heart
And the choir sings:

　　　　"Pour the oil and balm—"

And Cryzez prays:

　"O Lord of Light
　Whose reach makes distance myth,
　In whose abundant warmth
　The headlands of Cape Tollomon bask,"
　　　　"Over the dead—"
　"As all my life I dressed your leafy shrine,"
　　　　"Fire the cedar, fire the clove—"
　"Vouchsafe me this:"
　　　　"That the reek may lie—"
　"Absolve the Greeks,"
　　　　"And the savour lift—"

34

"Let the plague die,"
        "To Heaven, and to yourself."
"Amen."
        "Amen."

Were they deceived—or did
The bull consent with a shake of its head,
And the sunlight brighten, as Cryzez prayed?
Either way, the women sang:

"Child
      Child of Light
           We beg,"

Then the men:

"Heed the thirst in our song!"

"Lord
      Lord of Light
           We beg,"

Then the men:

"Feel the need in our song!"

And then:

"Lord
      Lord of Mice
           We pray,

"Let the plague die!
Let the plague die!"

They sang as one
And made the day divine.

    High smoke from oil-drenched bull tripes stood in Heaven.
Leaves of lean meat spat on the barbecues.
Silver took sea-dark wine from lip to lip.
Flutes. Anklets. Acorn bells. The shameless air.
Enough for all.
    And then, when simultaneously
The moon lit this side and the sun lit that
Side of the blades they lifted to salute
The Evening Star,
Safe in Apollo's custody they slept,
Sailed on Aurora's breath
Past that still sleepy turtle
Over the shaggy waves:

Heard that the plague had gone; were glad;
And said goodbye to one another as
Carrying their guns they ran across the plain to Troy.

But Achilles was not glad.
Each moment of each minute of the day
    "Let the Greeks die,
    Let them taste pain,"
Remained his prayer.
    And he for who
Fighting was breath, was bread,
Remained beside his fatal ships
Below the bay's west head,
And hurt his honour as he nursed his wrong.

GOD LIVES FOR EVER

Come quickly, child! There! There!
Salute Him with your eyes!
Brighter than day His shadow; silent as light
The footprint of His time-free flight
Down the Nile's length, across the Inland Sea
To Paradise Olympus where it rides
High on the snowy lawns of Thessaly,
And an unpleasant surprise is waiting for Him:

Thetis,
Wearing the beady look of motherhood,
Who starts right in:

"High King of Heaven, Whose Temple is the Sky,"
And then reminds Him of her conscientiousness;
Then (seating Him) of her enforced, demeaning coitus;
Then (as she keeps His hand) repeats
The promise He had given to her son:
    "If you, My Thetis' only child,
Choose to die young, by violence, alone,
Your honour will be recognized as best,
The best of bests,
The most astonishing that fame shall light,
Now, or in perpetuity."
    Then (twining her arms behind His knees)
She ends:
    "I must have Yes or No.
If Yes, repeat these words:
    'In honour of Your son
Whose honour has been blighted by his King,
In that that King has grabbed his honour she,
I will take Hector's part until
The Greeks stand soaked in blood from head to foot,

Crushed by an overwhelming Trojan victory.'
Then fatalize this promise with Your nod.
   If No, I am a lost bitch barking at a cloud."

   A crease has formed between God's eyes.
His silence hurts.
   Over His suppliant's tar-dark hair
He sees the ascension of the Evening Star
Beckon infinity. And says:

   "Goddess,
I am in trouble enough for savouring
Hector's high smoke.
   Next to her detestation of the Trojans,
My wife likes baiting Me:
   'So You have helped the Dribbler *again*,'
That is how Hera styles My favourite king,
Priam of windy Troy,
A stallion man—once taken for Myself—
Who serviced 50 strapping wives from 50 towns,
Without complaint—to unify My Ilium,
Though all she says is:
   'From where I sit Your city on the hill
Stinks like a brickfield wind.'
   I tell you, Thetis, Hera is Greek mad.
Unable to forget that Paris judged her less—
Nudely speaking—than Lady Aphrodite,
Hates My best boy, poor, pretty Trojan Ganymede—
And hates his city, too.
   Better leave now. Before she sees us talking.
Go. I nod. I answer Yes,"
Adding (but only to Himself): "In My own way—
And in My own good time."

   Then hitched His robe and strolled towards His court.

Hard as it is to change the interval
At which the constellations rise
And rise, against their background dark,
Harder by far, when God inclines His head
And in the overlight His hair
Flows up the towering sky,
To vary His clairvoyance. "Yes,"
He has said. Yes, it will be, and

Now,
In a hoop of tidal light,
The lesser gods observing His approach,
Approach, then wait, then bow, and then,
Lit by their deferential eyes,
Conduct the King of Heaven through His park,
Enthroning Him, and at His glance, themselves.
Except for her, His sister-wife, Queen Hera, who
Put her face close to His, and said:

"Warm Lord,
Have You ever seen a camel led by a crab?
If not, look here" (widening her eyes' malicious lazuli)
"And see Yourself.
   Not that I am surprised. Oh dear me, no.
Who mobilized the kings? Who sent the Fleet to Troy?
But once my back is turned—plot-plot, plan-plan,
Which I, of course, will be the last to hear of.
   That salty Thetis has been at Your knee.
Not a god's god, I know. But curved.
   What did You nod to as she left?
Just because all creation knows
Fig Paris with the curly-girly hair
Refused Athena and my humble self
Does not mean You can leave us ignorant."

"First Heart," God said, "do not forget
I am at least a thousand times
Raised to that power a thousand times
Stronger than you, and your companion gods.
What I have said will be, will be,
Whether you know of it, or whether not.
You are the god of married love and of fertility.
    So shut your mouth
Or I will kick the breath out of your bones."

And Hera did as she was told.

It was so quiet in Heaven that you could hear
The north wind pluck a chicken in Australia.

And as she reached her throne, she bit her tongue;
And when her son, the crippled Lord of Fire,
Came gimping up to her and said:
    "Mother?"
She turned away,
    "Mother?"
Then turned the other way, and would have said:
    "Not now.
I have enough to bear without the sight of you,"
Except her mouth was full of blood.
    "Mother,
You are quite right to be ashamed of me,
For you are large, and beautiful, while I
Am small and handicapped."
    And as she could not speak unless she gulped,
Just as she gulped, Hephaestus put
A jug that he had struck from frosted iron,
Then chased, in gold, with peonies and trout,
Into her hand, and said:
    "Forget God's words.

Spring kisses from your eyes.
Immortals should not quarrel over men."
Then, turning on his silver crutch
Towards his cousin gods, Hephaestus
Made his nose red, put on lord Nestor's voice,
And asked:
    "How can a mortal make God smile?"

(Two . . . three . . .)

"Tell Him his plans . . ."

    And as their laughter filled the sky
Hephaestus lumped away remembering how,
Angered at some mistake of his,
God tossed him out of Heaven into the void,
And how—in words so fair they shall forever be
Quoted in Paradise: "from morn
To noon he fell, from noon to dewy eve,
A summer's day; and with the setting sun
Dropped from the zenith like a falling star,
On Lemnos" in an arc that left
Him pincer-handed with crab-angled legs.

    And Hera recognized
The little jug's perfection with a smile,
As on God's arm, the lesser gods their train,
Starlit they moved across the lawns of Paradise,
Till them to Him, till Him to them, they bowed their might;
And soon, beside his lake-eyed queen,
Zeus lay asleep beneath the glamorous night.

    And so to Troy.

2

"Who's there?"
"Manto, sir."
"Manto?"
"Yes, sir. Your youngest son."

"Shine the light on your face.

"Come here.

"Now wipe my mouth.
No-no-no-no-no-no. From there.
I like a clean one every time."

Skirts graze.

"Ah, Soos . . ."

The curtain rings.

"Soos, this is my youngest son.
Soos is my herald. He must be . . ."
"80, Sire."
"And you?"
"11, sir.
Queen Neday's child."
"Of course.
Your mother was my eighth, full, wife.
Resigned to . . . Soos?"
"Lord Rebek, Sire.
Queen Hecuba's first nephew."

Others come.

"Now, Manto—tell me truthfully:
Have you killed your first Greek?"
    "I think so, sir. Today.
When the car stopped I shot one in the back."
    "Who had the reins?"
    "The Prince Aeneas, sir."

A pause. A look at Soos. And then
King Priam stands:
    Some eight foot six; indigo-skinned; his brush-thick hair
Vertical to his brow; blue-white:
Correctly known as the Great King of Troy;
Who says:

    "Aeneas is no more a prince than you.
He is Anchises' son, not mine.
Anchises cannot sire a prince.
Lords—yes; but princes—no.
    You, Manto, might—note I say *might*, Soos—"
    "Sire—"
    "Be king of Phrygiland one day, and tax
My hilltop cousin, lord Anchises, of some beef.
But that is all.
    And do not trust the gods too much, young man.
Gods fail their worshippers—but not themselves."

    "Your chair is here, Sire."

Like monumental wings
The doors that overlook the Acropolis' main court

Open onto the evening air
And Priam's portico.

And when his chair appears
(With four sons walking by each arm)
Neomab, Soos' next, declares:

"All rise for Priam, Laomedon's son,
Great King of Troy, the Lord of Ilium."
Old Priam seats his Council of 100 with his hand,
Gathers his strength, and cries:

"Where is my son? My only son?
I do not see my son! He has no twin!
Take all my sons, Achilles, but not him,"
But only to himself.

Aloud, he says:

"Blood-bound Allies—
Satraps of Thrace, of Bosphorus,
Marmarine Phrygiland and Hittite Anatolium Beyond;
    My wedded Ilians—
Cool Dardan North, dear Ida, dearest South;
    And you who come from Lycia and Cyprus:

"I reign with understanding for you all.
Trojan Antenor, being eldest, shall speak first.
    Our question is:
How can we win this war?"

"And I reply," Antenor says,
"How can we lose it?
    God's Troy has been besieged a dozen times
But never taken.

Your line goes back 900 years.
The Greeks have been here nine. Surely their chance
To take our city worsens in the tenth?"
    (Anchises' face is stone.
His kinsman, Pandar, spits.)
    "If we have difficulties, so do they;
If we are tired, so are they;
And we are tired at home. Behind our Wall.
    These are their facts:
Full tents, thin blankets, gritty bread.
    And one thing more: they have a case.
Their law of hospitality is absolute.
You are a guest, you are a king. The house is yours.
    Paris—may God destroy him—was Menelaos' guest
And Helen was/is Menelaos' wife.
He wants her back. Greece wants her treasure back.
Neither unreasonable demands.
Women are property for them.
And stolen property can be returned."

    Pandar would interrupt, but Meropt—
Aphrodité's priest—restrains him.

    "My King,
The winners of a war usually get
Something out of it.
    What will we get?
Their camp. Their ditch. And who wants those?
Only Lord Koprophag, the god of shit."

    Impatient now:

    "Stand Helen on a transport floored with gold,
And as they rumble through the Skean Gate

48

Let trumpets from the terracing
Bray charivari to her back's bad loveliness."

Applause.

And under it:
"Where can that Hector be?" the old King asks.
"On his way here, Sire. After sacrifice,"
Antenor ends:

"Achilles is no different from the rest.
Let him face stone. Our Wall. The death of Greece.
Keep its gates down and send our allies home.
Since men have lived, they lived in Troy.
Why fight for what is won?"

Now more—too much—applause,
Into the last of which:

"This is the why," Anchises, lord of Ida, said,
As Pandar and Didanam
(Pandar's bow-slave) helped, then held him up:

For 50 years ago
As he was swimming in Gargara's lake
My Lady Aphrodité glimpsed his pretty bum
And, while the spirits of the place looked on,
Had him on a mat of Darwin's clover.
That done,
She pushed his hair back off his brow,
Then took his hand and spoke to him by name:

"Anchises, I am fertile.
Our son, who you will call *Aeneas*, shall be king.

But cite our bond to anyone but him,
You will be paralyzed from the waist downwards."

Gods always ask too much.
Just as Anchises said, "This is the why,"
One day, to those who claimed that Mim,
A new-bought templemaid,
"Is good as Aphrodite," he said:
"She's not. I know, because I've had them both."
And as they shrilled, shrivelled from hip to foot.

Shrivelled or not:

"This is the why," Anchises said.
"Troy is not Ilium. And without Ilium
Troy will not last.
You say: 'Give Helen back, they will go home.'
O sorry orator, they have no home.
They are a swarm of lawless malcontents
Hatched from the slag we cast five centuries ago,
Tied to the whim of their disgusting gods,
Knowing no quietude until they take
All quiet from the world; ambitious, driven, thieves;
Our speech, like footless crockery in their mouths;
Their way of life, perpetual war;
Inspired by violence, compelled by hate;
To them, peace is a crime, and offers of diplomacy
Like giving strawberries to a dog.
Indeed, what sort of king excepting theirs
Would slit his daughter's throat to *start* a war?"

King Priam yawns.

"They must be beaten. Preferably, destroyed.
Return their she, her boxes, they will think:

'Ilium is weak'—and stay. Retain them, they will think:
'Ilium is fat'—and stay. As either way
They want your city whole; your wives,
Your stuff and stock, floodlit by fire, while they
Pant in their stinking bronze and lick their lips.
   Ask who you like from Troy Beyond:
The Dardanelles, Negara Point,
Arisbe, Hellespont, then south,
Hac, Paran, Tollomon, and from Kilikiax
Inland as far as Thebé-under-Ida,
Seaward to Chios and to Samothrace,
All say: 'For us, the time to die is ripe,' and have
Nothing to spare except their injuries.
'And where is Troy?' they ask. 'We paid her well.
Great Priam had our princess for a queen,
Now turns his back sending our allies home
As if Pe'leus' son was just a name.'

   "Ask Hector's wife. Andromache has lost
Her sire, King Etion, four brothers, and their town,
Shady Kilikiax, at Achilles' hands.
She will not underestimate the lad's ferocity.
   He is what they call Best. That is to say:
Proud to increase the sum of human suffering;
To make a wife, a widow; widows, slaves;
Hear, before laughter, lamentation;
Burn before build.
   Our only question is:
How best to kill him? Pandar has planned for that.
   The saying goes:
Not the dog in the fight but the fight in the dog.
And you, Antenor, like your sons, lack fight.
You speak from cowardice. You plan from fear."

   Then Pandar's "True!" was mixed with someone's "Shame . . ."

51

"Shame . . ." merged with "Answer him . . ." and "Stand . . ."
With "Heaven sent . . ." and ". . . let her go."
Their voices rising through the still, sweet air

As once, as tourists, my friends and I
Smoked as we watched
The people of the town of Skopje
Stroll back and forth across their fountained square,
Safe in their murmur on our balcony,
One dusk, not long before an earthquake tipped
Themselves and their society aside.

Now,
Almost by touch, the Council's tumult died, as
Gowned, down the flight of steps that join
The Temple's precinct to the court,
Surrounded by Troy's dukes, Prince Hector comes.

Whether it is his graceful confidence,
His large and easy legs and open look,
That lets him fortify your heart,
That makes you wish him back when he has gone,
Trusting oneself to him seems right; who has belief,
And your belief respected, where he stands.

"My son!"

No sound aside from Priam's cry, as Hector led
  Chylabborak,
Andromache's one brother left, King Etion's heir,
Across the courtyard; plus
  Aeneas,
Brave, level-headed, purposeful,
My Lady Aphrodité's child,

To whom Mount Ida's cowboys prayed:
    Troy's Lycian allies,
Gray, beside his prince, Sarpedon;
Anaxapart, Sarpedon's armourer:
    And more
As valiant, as keen for fame, the plumes of Ilium,
That you will meet before they die,
Followed their Hector up, onto the portico
Before the monumental wings, and stood
Around the King, who pulls his son's face down
And kisses it, even as he whispers:
    "Where have you *been*?"

And Hector lets the smile this brings
Fade from his lips, before he says:

    "My friends,
Your faces bear your thoughts. Change them for these:
    My name means 'He who holds.'
Troy; Ilium; Troy Beyond; one thing.
    The victory is God's.

    "Anchises harms the truth
By making it offensive.
    Antenor hides the truth
By making out that Greece has lost.
    True: Raphno of Tus arrived today
With fifteen hundred extra men.
    Yes, yes. And, yes: my father's relatives and I
Could hold Troy on our own.
    God break the charm of facts!
Excepting: we are tired of our Wall.
Of waking up afraid. Of thinking: Greece.
Your life in danger all your life. Never to rise alone

Before the birds have left their nests,
Then ride alone through sunlit, silent woods,
Deep snow to spring flowers in a single day,
And then, the sea . . .
   To miss these things,
When things like these are your inheritance,
Is shameful. As for my brother's wife,
She is no prisoner.

   "We are your heroes.
Audacious fameseekers who relish close combat.
Mad to be first among the blades,
Now wounded 50 times, stone sane.
And we will burn Greece out.
   Achilles' name, that turns you whiter than a wall,
Says this: although his mother is a god,
He is a man, and like all men, has just one life,
Can only be in one place at one time.
   It will be plain to see whose part Heaven takes;
If God guides Hector's spearcast, or if not;
If God is pleased with Hector, or if not;
If not, it is a manly thing, an honourable thing
To die while fighting for one's country.

"Fate's sister, Fortune, favours those who keep their nerve.
I know it is the plain that leads
Us to their ships, and them into the sea.
And when God shows the moment we should strike
I will reach out for it.
   But I—
Not you, Anchises, and not you, Antenor—
Will recognize that moment when it comes.

   "All captains to their towers.
Sleep tight. But do not oversleep."

Did our applause delay him?
Out of the corner of his eye, Chylabborak
Sees a strange herald cross to Neomab and Soos,
Then Soos make not-now signs to Neomab,
Then Neomab, apologizing with a shrug,
Go to Priam and his dukes, who ring him, and
(While our silence holds) listen, then nod.
Then face ourselves as Soos declares:

"Cryzez of Tollomon sends this news:
Achilles has walked out on Greece.
Tomorrow he sails home."

"So I am right!"
"So I am right!"
In unison, Antenor and Anchises called.
And so again, as in that fountained square,
"True," "Shame," "Right," "Answer him," and ". . . let her go,"
Became the cross-talk of their dark, that grew
Slowly and slowly less, until
All were as quiet as children drawing.

Then Hector said:

"Listen to me, and take my words to heart.
This changes nothing.
I lift my hands to God,
Whose voice knows neither alien heart nor land.
He is my word, my honour, and my force.
I shall bury Greece."

And went.

Immediately below the parapet
Of Troy's orbital Wall, wide, house-high terraces
Descend like steps until they mill
The flagstone circus ringing the Acropolis,
Whose acre top supports palace and palace walk,
Rooms by the flight where Priam's 50 sons
Slept safe beside their wives before Greece came.
    God's Temple faces south.
And over there (beyond the altar lights and colonnades
Of Lord Apollo and of Lady Aphrodite)
Notice the stairs that wind
Onto a balcony where Helen stands
And says:

    "They want to send me back."
And (taking a pastry snail from a plate
Inlaid with tortoise-shell) Paris replies:

    "Heaven sent you here. Let Heaven send you back."

    And as they drive through Troy
Pandar assures Aeneas: "I
Never miss. Heaven aims my bow.
My future is assured."

    Go to the flat-topped rock's west side and see
Andromache touch Hector's shoulder:

    "Love,
I am a good and patient wife.
I speak the truth. My father was a King.
Yet when he slaughtered him

56

Achilles did not rubbish Etion's corpse
But laced him in his plate and lifted him,
As tenderly I do our son, onto his pyre,
And let our 12-year-olds plant cypresses
Around his cairn before he burnt
Leafy Kilikiax and led them to his ships.
    Distrust cold words.
Friendship is yours, and openheartedness.
I hear your step—I smile behind my veil.
To measure you, to make your clothes,
Your armour, or to forge your blades,
Is privilege in Troy. You keep your word.
You fear disgrace above defeat. Shame before death.
And I have heard your bravery praised
As many times as I have dried my hands.
Be sure of it—as you are sure of me.
As both of us are sure
Courage can kill as well as cowardice,
Glorious warrior."

    Then as they walk along the pergola
Towards the tower of the Skean Gate,
Shadowed by Rimph and Rimuna, her maids,
Her wedding present from Chylabborak,
Both honoured to sleep Hector, if he chose:

    "Half Troy is under 25, my love.
Half of the rest are wounded, widowed, old.
Hush . . ." raising her finger to his lips,
"Why else does Prince Aeneas take a boy
As young as Manto in his car?"

    "Aeneas is my business."

Silence.

Then:

"My lord, you never yet
Treated me like a woman.
    Do not start now.
Your family quarrels are your own," and walked
Before her skirts that trailed along the floor
Before him through the horseshoe arch
Into the tower's belvedere, retied
The threads of her veil at the back of her head,
Smiled Rimuna and Rimph away, then said:
    "Dearest, nearest soul I know,
You hesitate to fight below your strength.
Short work, therefore, to needle Hector with the thought
It was the weakness of the Greeks and not his strength
That kept them out, that kept them down, that sent them home.
But those who say so preach: not prove.
    Why, sir, even if you sent
Sarpedon, Gray, Anaxapart
Back home to Lycia, Aeneas to his hills,
Prior to shouldering Agamemnon's race
Into the Dardanelles, alone,
Those propagandists would not change their tune.
    Day after day I wash Greek blood off you;
It teaches me that Greece is not so far,
And not so strange, to be exempt exhaustion.
    Send Helen back.
Let her establish a world-record price.
Desire will always be her side-effect.
And Achilleus is out.
    O love, there is a chance for peace.
Take it. We all die soon enough."

Hieee . . . Daughter of Etion,
From diadem past philtrum on to peeping shoes

You show another school of beauty.
  And while he looked
Over the Trojan plain towards the Fleet,
Your Hector said:
  "I know another way,"
As moonlight floods the open sky.

3

Now all creation slept
Except its Lord, the Shepherd of the Clouds,
Who lay beside His sister-wife
With Thetis on His mind.

So to a passing Dream He said:

"Go to the Fleet.
Enter its King.
Tell him this lie:
    'Strike now, and you will win.
God's lake-eyed queen has charmed the gods
And thrown a great nought over Troy.' "

Disguised as Nestor's voice, the Dream
Sank into Agamemnon's upside ear, and said:

"Lord of the Shore, the Islands, and the Sea,
You know my voice. You know I speak the truth.
    You are God's King. He pities you. And is,
As always, on your side. These are His words:
    'War-weary as you are,
Strike now, hero and host, as one, and you will win.
My lake-eyed queen has charmed the gods
And drawn a great nought over Troy.' "

And as its host awakened, the Dream died.

Heralds to Agamemnon's tent.
Bright apricot rifts the far black.

They bow.

"Fetch my great lords.
Then have your less assemble Greece."

And as Talthibios did,
Dawn stepped barefooted from her lover's bed
And shared her beauty with the gods,
Who are as then; and with ourselves, as now.

Outside.

Pylos and Salamis,
Crete, Sparta, Tiryns, Ithaca, and Macedon.

Formidable.

Even a god would pause.

But not himself:

"I have important news.
An hour ago,
Dressed in your voice, dear lord of Sandy Pylos,
God came to me and said:
'Make total war today, hero and host, as one,
Troy will be yours by dusk.'"

The dawn wind pats their hair.

Odysseus gazes at his big left toe.
His toe. Until Idomeneo said:

"Then you awoke, my Lord."
"I did.
And sent for you at once."

A pause.

Then Nestor said:
"You say it had my voice?"
"It did."
"My normal voice?"
"Your normal voice."
"The voice that you hear now?"
"As now."

Nobody speaks.

"Well?"

Nobody.

Along the beach-head's eastern reach
Stentor is assembling Ajax' men.

Then Diomed:

"My Lord, excuse my age.
Young as I am I wish to ask you if,
By 'as one,' by 'total war,' you mean us lords to fight
Beside the less?"

"I do."

"My lord, I am the child of kings."

"And we are not?"

"My lord, my uncle, Meleager, slew
The mammoth hog that devastated Calydon.
My father died while fighting for your own
Against the eyeless tyrant, Oedipus of Thebes,
And his incestine heirs. In Argolis
My family lands defend the frontiers of your own.
Perhaps the Daughter Prince will offer me
A glorious death beneath the walls of Troy,
Or if that is presumptuous, then at least
Wounds, without which no hero is complete,
A trumpet played into a drain.
    Of course you are delighted by the thought
Of taking Troy without Achilles,
And that our herd must fill the gap
That righteous lord has left.
    But, sir,
Why should I fight alongside my inferiors?
The herd is cowardly; a show of dirty hands;
Slop for Thersites' scrag; that have as gods
Some rotten nonsense from the East.
    Bred from the instruments of those
Our ancestors evicted or destroyed,
Bronze is for them to polish, not to wear.
Better be born a woman, leaky, liking to lose,
Or a decent horse, than one of them.
Bitter but better, fetch Pe'leus' son,
Tiptoe around him, pick one's moment, plead,
Than share our triumph with our trash."

Everyone looks in a different direction.

Then Nestor said:

"Paramount Agamemnon,
Had anyone except yourself so dreamt
I would have begged him not to mention it.
But as things are, we will inspire
Both lords and less to fight for you.
    As for yourself, young sir,
Remember that I fought beside your father.
He would say this:
    What Heaven has ordered, Heaven can change.
If God says total war, total it is."

See sheep in Spain: the royal flock
Taking five days to pass you as they wind
White from their winter pasture, up
Onto the Whitsun prairie of Castile
And wig its brow, then weed, with even pace,
That sunny height, meanwhile their collies seem
To chase the passing sky.

    Muter than these
But with as irresistible a flow
The army left its lines and walked
Over the slipways, in between the keels,
Along the camp's main track beside the ditch,
And settled round the common sand.

All still.

Talthibios:

"Absolute silence for the Son of Atreus,
Agamemnon of Mycenae, King of kings."

"Soldiers!" he said.
"Dressed in lord Nestor's words, our Lord and God,
Whose voice dethrones the hills,
Entered my head an hour before the dawn.
    These were His words:
    'Yours is the greatest army ever known.
Assault Troy now. Hero and host. As one.
And by this time tomorrow all its flesh
And all its fat will be your own to stow
As you prepare to sail for home; for I, your God,
As I have ever been, am on your side.'"

    After nine years,
No throat that did not ache, then would not cheer,
Hearing such things.
    Yet as hope rose, so did Thersites,
And in his catchy whine said:

    "King,
God may be on your side, but if He is on mine
Why is Troy still standing over there?"
    Then capped our titter: "How—
Us being the greatest army ever known,
Outnumbering Troy by three to two—
Have we not won the war?
    As for our sailing home,
Review the Fleet with me—but, O my Lord,
Please do not fart. You are a powerful man
And perished sails blow out. Then when,
Us having scanned the shrouds, my Lord,
You stroke your chin and rest your expert eye,
Resist the urge to lean against a mast,

They are so rotten you can push a walking-stick
Clean through them."

"True."
"True."

As he wades through our knees
Down to the front.

Will he step out?

He does.

He says:

"Son of Atreus, you astonish me.
You ask the Greeks to fight in a main vein for you,
Opposing Gray and duke Chylabborak, hand to hand,
Yet rob the man our victory depends on.
    What do you want?
More bronze? *More* shes? Your tents are full. And yet,"
Turning to us, "who was the last man here to hear
Lord Agamemnon of Mycenae say: 'Have this'—
Some plate—'brave fighter' or 'share this'—
A teenage she.
    One thing is sure,
That man would be surprised enough to jump
Down the eye-hole of his own knob.

    "Why laugh?
Achilles is not laughing.
The lords have let their King grab his mint she.
Achilles has been hurt. Achilles shows restraint.
If he did not"—back to the King—"my Lord,
You would be dead."

Our shoulders rise and fall.
Something is going to happen. Soon.
　　And from the middle sand Thersites shouts:

"Thick shes!—*I* have important news:
God is on Atreus' Troy-mortgaged side,
And on his shackled captains' side.
　　Comrades in arms with God, why,
Such lordies can take Ilium alone,
Not share their triumph with their trash.
　　So, timid nymphs, things to be stolen, tea
To his tablespoons, as he needs us
No more than our Achilles needs
Snot on his spearpole—we are free to go.
Go where? Go home," and here some run to him:
"Go home at once. The host. As one,"
And raise his hands: "By noon we can be rowing,
Seeing this hopeless coast fade,"
Hold his fists high, as:

　　"Home . . .
　　Home . . .
　　Home . . ."

We answered him,
All standing now, beneath:

　　"Home . . .
　　Home . . ."

　　All darkened by that word,
　　　As sudden gusts
Darken the surface of a lake; or passing clouds,
A hill; or both, a field of standing corn,
　　We flowed

Back through the ships, and lifted them;
Our dust, our tide; and lifted them; our tide;
Hulls dipping left; now right; our backs, our sea;
Our masts like flickering indicators now;
Knees high; "Now lift . . ." knocked props; "Now lift again . . ."
And our relief, our sky; our liberty;
As each enjoyed his favourite thoughts; his plans;
And to a Trojan watcher we appeared
Like a dinghy club, now moored on mud;
Now upright on bright water; and now gone.

So Greece near crowned its fate and came safe home,
Except the gods,
Whose presence can be felt,
For whom a thousand years are as a day,
Said: "No."

Quicker than that,
At Hera's nod Athena stood beside Odysseus
And ran her finger down his spine.
Aoi!—see him move,
Taking his driver, Bombax, into their flight
Like flight; and saying: "Wrap that dog," hand
Bombax his crimson boat-cloak, and then leap
Onto a tilting deck and spread
His big bare feet, and cast
His landslide voice across the running beach.
And she,
Teenage Athena of the tungsten eyes,
Divided lord Odysseus' voice
Into as many parts as there were heads.
So each lord heard:

"You are the best. You hold your ground.
You were born best. You know you are the best
Because you rule. Because you take, and keep,
Land for the mass. Where they can breed. And pray. And pay
You to defend them. You to see custom done.
What cannot be avoidcd, you endure.

So that mass heard
Odysseus' charming voice:
   "Be fair. The plague has gone."
His wise:
   "Even if all Thersites says is true . . ."
His firm:
   "The lords are going to stay."
His practical:
   "You know the sea?"
His hard:
   "Kakhead, get back into your place."

Hearing these things, the fighters slowed,
Looked at each other's faces, looked away,
Looked at the water, then about, and turned,
Re-turned, and turned again,
Chopping and changing as a cliff-stopped sea's
First wave slaps back into the next,
That slaps the next, that slaps.

Bombax has got
Thersites in Odysseus' cloak
And roped it round.
   And as he humps it up the beach,
It starts; and those who watch it going by
Feel scared.

There is a kind of ocean wave
Whose origin remains obscure.
Such waves are solitary, and appear
Just off the cliff-line of Antarctica
Lifting the ocean's face into the wind,
Moistening the wind that pulls, and pulls them on,
Until their height (as trees), their width
(As continents), pace that wind north for 7,000 miles.

And now we see one!—like a stranger coast
Faring towards our own, and taste its breath,
And watch it whale, then whiten, then decay:
Whose rainbow thunder makes our spirits leap.

Much like its suds the shamefaced Greeks returned
Along the many footpaths of the camp
And ringed the common sand.

Some minutes pass.

And then,
With his big, attractive belly rounded out
And just a trace of dark grey hair
Ascending and descending to his cloth

Odysseus (small but big)

Half casually

Holding a broomstick cane

Strolled over to the still
Occasionally jerking item
Bombax had dropped onto the sand.

Then:
Stoop—
Grip—
And . . .
Hup!—
Odysseus slewed Thersites out:
Who knelt; who tried to slip his gag; then did.

   "Speak out," Odysseus said.
"Think of your crowd.
As they brought you to life,
Because of you they see themselves
As worthy of respect. To have a voice.

   "No?

   "Not a word.

   "You must have something to complain about?"

No sound.

   "Then, there, old soldier, I can be of help."

   And raised the cane and gave Thersites' neck,
Nape, sides, back, butt, stroke after slow, accurate stroke,
And pain, lewd pain, a weeping pain, your smash-hit,
High-reliability, fast-forward pain.

   Then passed the cane to Bombax,
Took back his cloak, helped poor Thersites up, and said
Softly to him, but also to them all:

   "God *is* on Agamemnon's side.
Fear God—fear him. Fear him—fear me. Fear me—

And those like me—and save yourselves.
    As for Achilles: Sir,
That lord would sooner cut his hand off than shake yours.
Let Panachea hear your voice again
And I will thrash you, bare, across the bay
From Ajax' to Achilles' ships—and back."

    As for Thersites
Our shoulders parted, and he sat
Touching his welts with one
And with the knuckles of his other hand
Wiping his tears away.

    And as it is with fighters,
Shamed as we were a laugh or two went up:

    "He went too far."
    "Admit Odysseus talks sense."
    "Shush . . . shush . . ."

For having joined the greater lords
And, at Agamemnon's nod, taken the mace:

    "Odysseus is going to speak."

Some say the daylight sharpens where he stands
Because Athena guards him:

    "So she does."

    And so we see her now,
Like an unnamed, intelligent assistant,
Standing a touch behind him, on the left.

    Talthibios says:

"That those far off may hear as well
As those close to, full silence for
Prudent Odysseus, the lord of Ithaca."

Who keeps his eyes well down
And turns his words towards King Agamemnon.

Gulls.

"True King," Odysseus said,
"No Greek believes more firmly than myself
That all occasions are at God's command.
    As God gave you, our King of kings, to us,
So you are given the best of all we take,
And you, through Heaven, ensure due custom done.

    "Remember then"—turning his voice on us—
"You who believe the last thing that you heard;
Who tell yourselves you think, when you react;
Captains in camp, but cowards on the plain;
Keen to be off, but frightened of the sea—
You are not King. You never shall be King.
You see a hundred Agamemnons. God sees one,
And only one. Who bears the mace. Who speaks His word.
Who cares for us.
    So keep your democratic nonsense to yourselves,
And when your betters speak to you—obey."

    Idomeneo twists a fig
Off Merionez' bunch.

    "At the same time, we veterans who recognized
Queen Hera's voice in Agamemnon's call
Are sure Lord Agamemnon knows how hard it is
For anyone—lord, less—to be away from home,

Stuck on some island, say, no wife, no she,
Even for a month, let alone years.
    But as we know this, so we know
The world has no time for a King whose fighters leave him.
Or would you have Obstropolous Thersites for your King?"

    Swifts flit from spear to spear.

    "Of course we are impatient.
That is Greek.
    Yet, as it is wrong
To be found drunk at sacrifice; wrong
Not to hold your father in your arms;
Consider how much worse would be to row
With bowed heads home
Over the open graveyard of the sea
And then walk emptyhanded through the door?

    "Those with the Fleet at Aulis will recall
King Agamemnon sacrificed his child,
Iphigeneia, plus 50 bulls,
For us to have flat seas and following winds.
And when their throats hung wide
And we were kneeling by the smoky spring—
Beneath its cedar tree, before its stone,
A slug-white thigh-thick python slid
Out of the ferns that bibbed the stone,
Then glided through the lake of votive blood
And up into the tree and searched its leaves.
    Eight fledgling sparrows chirruped in those leaves.
And, as we watched, the python vacuumed them up,
Then schlooped their mother off the air,
Tainting our sacrifice—or so we thought.
    However, as the great snake fawned
And periscoped above the cedar's crown

77

God stared into its eyes. And it was stone.
White stone. Figured with gold. Tall. Smooth white stone.
A thing of beauty from a loathsome thing."

"Indeed . . ."

"Then Calchas, full of fate"
(Sighting his finger on that seer),
"Opened those omens with these words . . ."
(Who swallows, stands, then recapitulates:)

"The time has come for Greece to praise its God.
What we have seen means this:
   Eight young—eight years before the Wall.
But when their father's summer ninth has come,
Victory over Hector will be ours."

"This is that summer," lord Odysseus called
(Leaving the anxious Calchas on his feet).
   "To waste our King's dream is to scorn our dead.
So we strike now. Hero and host. As one.
Take Troy by total war. Then sail safe home."

These were Odysseus' words.
And as he sat, Greece rose and roared:

"Troy . . . Troy . . . Troy . . . Troy . . ."

Echoing in the hulls, along the dunes,
While Agamemnon stood:
Then, when they settled, sat. And said:

"I thank the Lord that king Odysseus has found the words
To bring Greece to its senses, and hope it manages to keep them.

Similar silliness
Made me begin the quarrel with Achilles
About some foreign she.
    Well, well. God's ways are strange.
    So no regrets.
This is the morning of the day
Whose dusk will see Troy won.
    The lords will join me for the battle sacrifice.
The less will eat and arm.
    Never forget that we are born to kill.
We keep the bloodshed to the maximum.
Be confident that I shall plant my spear
Deep in the back of any hero who mistakes
His shieldstrap for a safety belt, his feet
For running shoes, for soon, with God our Father's help,
Each one of you will have a Trojan she
To rape and rule, to sell or to exchange,
And Greece will be revenged for Helen's wrong."

    And why, I cannot say, but while he sat
Our answering cheer was like the wave foreseen,
When, crest held high, it folds
And down cloud thunders up the shaken coast.

A hundred deep
The lords surround their lords:
    Merionez, Idomeneo's next,
His eyes the colour of smoked glass;
    Odysseus, unthanked—but unsurprised;
    Ajax (of course), and standing by him
Little Ajax—like a side of beef—
His brother by a purchased she;

By him their cousin, Teucer;
Diomed, short, slight, just 17;
Thoal of Macedon, his hair like coconut,
Who always knows exactly what to do;
And Menelaos, silent, doubtful, shy,
Watching lord Nestor lead a huge red hog
With gilded tusks into the ring,
Conscious his brother has supplied the sacrifice,
And, as the King, has worries of his own.

And all their world is bronze;
White bronze, lime-scoured bronze, glass bronze,
As if,
Far out along some undiscovered beach
A timeless child, now swimming homewards out to sea,
Has left its quoit.

Agamemnon dips his hands in holy water.
Talthibios, having scattered barley on the ground,
Snips a tuft from the hog's nape,
Waits for the breeze to nudge it off his palm
Into the fire: looks at his King,

Who prays:

"Force Lord of Heaven,
O Dark, Immortal Breath,
Hold back the night until I break
Into Hector's body with my spear,
Fill Troy with fire,
And give its sobbings to the wind."

"Pae'an . . ."
"Vouchsafe us Troy."

Curls of high smoke
As if the air was water.
    The heroes kneel. Then lift their palms.
King Agamemnon draws his knife. Its point goes in.

    Ah me . . .
God took your hog but spiked your prayer.
    Futureless spoons, His name is everywhere,
His name is everywhere. And when the barbecue
Of fat-wrapped thigh-cuts topped with lights,
And from its silver, sea-dark wine had crossed your lips,
Lord Nestor stood, and said:

    "Today will be our longest day." (But he was wrong.)
    "The engineers will top
The rampart with a palisade
One pitchlength shipward from the ditch,
Which, while Thetis' son is not our front,
Will be our back.
    God stop that any Greek,
Wherever from, whatever place he holds, should die
Without hard fighting and renown.
    So no more talk.
    The King will arm. You lords will join the host,
Answering our clear-voiced heralds as they call—
From mountain fastness, riverside, or lake,
Farm, forest, lido, hinterland, or shore,
Pasture or precinct, well or distant wall,
By father's name, or family name, or lord's,
The long-haired Greeks to battle, with this cry:

    "Lead on, brave King, as you have led before,
    And we shall follow."

Immediately
Wide-ruling Agamemnon's voices called
Greece to its feet, and set it on the move;
    And as they moved,
To stunt-hoop tambourines and trumpet drums,
The Daughter Prince, ash-eyed Athena, flew
Her father's awning, called the Aegis, blue,
Broad as an upright sky, a second sky
Over their shoulders rippling estuary,
    And turned the pad
Of tassel-ankled feet, the scrape of chalk
On slate, of chariot hubs, back on itself
And amplified that self; contained its light;
Doubled its light; then in that blinding trapped
Man behind man, banner behind raised banner,
My sand-scoured bronze, my pearl and tortoise gold,
And dear my God, the noise!
As if the hides from which 10,000 shields were made
Came back to life and bellowed all at once.
    See how the hairy crests fondle each other onwards as
From hill and valley, well and distant wall,
All those Queen Hera mobilized
Moved out, moved on, and fell in love with war again.

        "KING!" "KING!"

    As shining in his wealth, toting the solar mace,
Thighs braced against his chariot's wishbone seatstays,
The Shepherd of the Host,
Lord of the Shore, the Islands, and their Sea,
God's Agamemnon in his bullion hat
Drove down their cheering front.

        "KING!" "KING!"

20,000 spears at ninety, some
scaffolding poles, full-weight, to thrust,
        moving towards Troy; some light,
surveyor rods, to throw;
10,000 helmets—mouth-hole, eye-hole
(like a turtle's skull), chin-strapped or strapless;
        "Move . . . Move . . ."
5,000 crests—T, fore-and-aft, forward curving
(though either will do), some half-moon war-horns;
        "Move . . ."
shields: posy, standard, 8-oval-8 or "tower,"
two-to-six plyhide, some decked with bronze;
bows: single curve, lip-curved, lip-curved with reflex tip
(tested, found arrow-compatible);
        "Keep up, there . . ."
blades: short, long, leaf, stainless,
haft-rivets set square :: triangular ∴ with rat-tailed tangs
(these from Corfiot workshops, those imported);
        "Chariots!"
axes (single and double headed) slings (plus stones),
good (hay-fed) car-mares, each with her rug
(these double as body bags);
ships: long, black, swift, how many, how full;
400 tons of frozen chicken—their heads a world away;
a green undercoat;
and reaching the top of the swell in the plain:
        "*Now* see the Wall."
barbs, barbs plus spur, spades, beaded quivers,
body-paint, paste flecked with mica, arm-rings,
chapati-wrapped olives, hemmed sheepskins
(in case it gets cold without warning)

        "KING!" "KING!"

hear the high-pitched roar of armour advancing,
birth bronze, dust bronze, surgical bronze,
mirror bronze, cup bronze, dove
(seven parts copper to one part tin)
down the low hill towards Troy.

The Husbands

"A drink! A toast!   *To those who must die.*"

"On my land, before my sons,
Do you accept this womb, my daughter, Helen, as your wife?"
"I do."
"Her young shall be your own?"
"They shall."
"You will assume her gold?"
"I will."
"Go. You are his. Obey him. And farewell."

Troy.
The Acropolis.
The morning light behind the Temple's colonnade,
Then through that colonnade, Hector of Troy,
Towards his mass of plate-faced warriors:
    And your heart leaps up at the sight of him,
And wonders of courage are secretly sworn
As he says:

    "Torches and Towers of Troy, the Greeks are lost.
They dare not wait, but are ashamed to go
Home in their ships to their belovèd land
Without our city stowed. Therefore for them:
This desperate advance. Therefore for us:
Trumpets at sunrise from the mountain tops!

87

Our gods are out! Apollo! Aphrodite! so close,
You taste the air, you taste their breath, a loving breath
That shall inspire such violence in us,
Dear hearts, full hearts, strong hearts, courageous hearts,
Relaxing on our spears among their dead,
'*Heaven fought for us, 100 bulls to Heaven,*'
Will be our pledge.
   I put my hands in yours.
Prepare to be in constant touch with death
Until the Lord our God crowns me with victory."

   These were his words,
And knowing what you do you might have said: "Poor fool . . ."
Oh, but a chilly mortal it would be
Whose heart did not beat faster in his breast
As Quibuph set the cloche-faced gull-winged gold
Helmet with vulture feather plumes on Hector's head,
And Hector's trumpeter, T'lesspiax,
Set the long instrument against his lips
And sent:
   "Reach for your oars!"
   "Reach for your oars!"
In silver out across the plain:
And then, as Hector shook his shoulders out, again,
Again, as Hector's throng gave a great shout of rage
As down from the Acropolis they flowed
And through the streets they pressed.

   Breakfast in Heaven.
Ambrosia alba wreathed with whispering beads.
   "*In the Beginning there was no Beginning,*
And in the End, no End," sing the Nine to the Lord,

As Hera's eyebrows posit: *"Now?"*
And now Athene goes.

T hink of those fields of light that sometimes sheet
Low-tide sands, and of the panes of such a tide
When, carrying the sky, they start to flow
Everywhere, and then across themselves:
Likewise the Greek bronze streaming out at speed,
Glinting among the orchards and the groves,
And then across the plain—dust, grass, no grass,
Its long low swells and falls—all warwear pearl,
Blue Heaven above, Mount Ida's snow behind, Troy inbetween.
And what pleasure it was to be there! To be one of that host!
Greek, and as naked as God, naked as bride and groom,
Exulting for battle! lords shouting the beat out
   "One—"
Keen for a kill
   "Two-three"
As our glittering width and our masks that glittered
Came over that last low rise of the plain   and

   "Now"

(As your heart skips a beat)

   "See the Wall."

And you do.

It is immense.

So high

89

So still

It fills your sight.

And not a soul to be seen, or a sound to be heard,
Except, as on our thousands silence fell,
The splash of Laomedon's sacred springs,
One hot, one cold, whose fountains rise or die
Within a still day's earshot of the Wall
And inbetween whose ponds the Skean road
Runs down beneath the zigzags of God's oak
Until, under the gate of the same name,
It enters Troy, majestic on its eminence.

Within: Prince Hector's mass,
Without: a pause, until
Paramount Agamemnon, King of kings,
The Lord of Mainland and of Island Greece,
Autarch of Tiryns and Mycenae, looked
Now right, now left,
Then at the Wall, then into Heaven, and drew his sword.
And as he drew, Greece drew.
And this dis-scabbarding was heard in Troy
Much like a shire-sized dust-sheet torn in half.
    A second pause. And then
At Agamemnon's word the Greeks moved on
Down the low hill to Troy
As silently as if they walked on wool.

    The gates swing up:
The Skean, the Dardanian, the South.

    Hector: "Not yet."

"Not yet."

Then:

"Now."

Think of the noise that fills the air
When autumn takes the Dnepr by the arm
And skein on skein of honking geese fly south
To give the stateless rains a miss:
So Hector's moon-horned, shouting dukes
Burst from the tunnels, down the slope,
And shout, shout, shout, smashed shouted shout
Backward and forth across the sky;
While pace on pace the Greeks came down the counterslope
With blank, unyielding imperturbability.

25 yards between them.

20.

Then,
As a beam before its source,
Hector sprang out and T'd his spear; halted his lines;
Then lowered it; and stood alone before the Greeks.

King Agamemnon calls:
"Silent and still for Hector of the soaring war-cry,
The irreplaceable Trojan."

Then hands removed Prince Hector's shield, his spear,
And all Greece saw his massive frame, historical
In his own time, a giant on the sand, who said:

"Greek King: I speak for Ilium.

We have not burned you in your ships.
You have not taken Troy. Ten years have passed.
Therefore I say that we declare a truce,
And having sworn before the depths of Heaven to keep our word,
Here, in God's name, between our multitudes,
I will fight any one of you to death.
 And if I die" (this said within an inch of where he will)
"My corpse belongs to Troy and to Andromache;
My body-bronze to him who takes my life;
And to you all, Helen, your property, who was no prisoner, with her gold.
 And if I live: my victim's plate shall hang
Between the columns of Apollo's porch on our Acropolis,
But you may bear his body to the coast
And crown it with a shaft before you sail
Home in your ships to your belovèd land
With nothing more than what you brought to mine.
 Pick your best man. Commit yourselves to him.
Be sure that I am big enough to kill him
And that I cannot wait to see him die.
Then in their turn, faring from world to world across our sea,
Passengers who come after us will remark:
'That shaft was raised for one as brave and strong
As any man who came to fight at Troy,
Saving its Prince, Hector,
Superb on earth until our earth grows cold,
Who slaughtered him.' Now who will that Greek be?"

 Answer him, Greece!

 But Greece has lost its voice.

 Thoal is studying the sun-dried heads
And chariot chassis fastened to the Wall.

 Titters from Troy.

Then cannon off lord Menelaos': "Me."
"No.   Hector will kill you," from his brother.

Yet he has gone—how could he not?—out
Onto the nearside ground. Alone.

But someone is already there.

Odysseus. The king of Ithaca.

History says,
Before Odysseus spoke he seemed to be,
Well . . . shy—shuffling his feet, eyes down—the usual things.
However, once it passed his teeth, his voice possessed
Two powers: to charm, to change—
Though if it were the change that made the charm
Or charm the change, no one was sure.

The sun gains strength.
Thoal has taken Menelaos' hand.

Odysseus:

"Continuing and comprehensive glory to you both,
Hector, the son of Priam, King of Troy,
Agamemnon, the son of Atreus, my King.
And to us all.

"I dare not speak for Heaven,
But as our Lord, the Shepherd of the Clouds,
Has honoured us by following our war,
Now, through Prince Hector's lips He seems to say:
   Let the world flow through Priam's gates again
And Greece return to Greece with all debts paid.
   Lords of the earth,

We are God's own. Our law is His. Is force.
What better way to end this generous war
Than through the use of force—but force in small:
Not, all to die for one, but one for all.
    The proverb says:
The host requires the guest to make himself at home.
The guest remembers he is not.
This is the reason why no Greek
Dared to pre-empt lord Menelaos' right
To take Prince Hector's challenge, even if—
Greece having sworn to keep the word it gives—
The Lord our God returns him to Oblivion.
    Why wait, then?
    Comrades in arms, here is the why:
Hector has fought and fought, has given blood, and now—
Breathtaking grace—offers his armour and his life to end
The hostilities he did not cause.
    Fighters! Brave souls! Surely that is enough?
Even lord Schlacht, the hate-hot god of war, says: True,
It is enough.
    So who should Menelaos fight . . . ? My friends,
Your silence says: Only fools state the obvious.
And as there's no fool like an old fool, so
It falls to me to state it:

    "Paris.

    "The handsome guest . . ."

    "Yes."

    ". . . the one who started it . . ."

    "Yes." "Yes." (and rising)

"among us on the plain here . . ."

"Yes!"

". . . who else to face the man whose property he stole,
Soft in his bed up there on the Acropolis?
Paris, with his undoubted stamina,
Will give our Greek a long and vicious fight to death."

"Ave!"

"What fitter culmination to our war,
Or climax apter it to end?"

A beat, and then
The great assembly pleased itself with cheers
That bumped the Wall, and coasted on
Over the foothills and the moony dunes,
The woods and waterfalls of Ida, on—
Bearing their favourite thoughts and plans,
Their *"Peace for me,"* their joy at going home.

"Find him."

No need for that. At Hector's word,
Like dancers on a note, the shields divide,
And there, chatting among themselves, we see
Prince Paris' set; Pandar, his fan; Tecton,
The architect who built his fatal ships—
With Paris in their midst.

Napoleon's Murat had 50 hats
And 50 plumes each 50 inches high

And 50 uniforms and many more
Than 50 pots of facial mayonnaise
Appropriate to a man with tender skin;
He also had 10,000 cavalry,
Split-second timing, and contempt for death.
So Providence—had he been born
Later and lowlier—might well have cast Prince Paris.
   The centuries have not lied:
Observe the clotted blossom of his hair,
Frost white, frost bright—and beautifully cut,
Queen Aphrodité's favourite Ilian.
And though his hands are only archer's hands
(Half Hector's size) his weight half Hector's weight,
He is as tall as Hector (8'9"),
And as he walks towards him, note his eyes
As once his father's were: pure sapphire.

   They have not spoken for five years.

   "Oh, there you are."
(Blowing a speck off his brother's plate.)
"The womanizing smirk who took their queen.
Troy's heir. A picker. Picking one
Whose owners live for nothing except war.
Our specialist. Nice. Nice.
The world says yes to you before you ask.
Your laughter pardons your betrayals in advance.
What does he do at dusk when other souls
Beg God to see them through the night?
The same thing that he does at dawn.
Your hair, your voice, your dancing, your guitar.
   Beautiful filth, you must be pleased.
It is a long time since you had the chance
To be the man you were the day you brought her

And them ashore, brought her, and them, ashore at Abydos,
Now burnt, brought her to Troy—still standing, just—
Via Arisbe, Lia'gal'ia, Paran:
Burnt, demolished, burnt. Beautiful filth,
Here is your opportunity to be that man again
Before you die, courtesy her first husband, I should think:
Take it, or I shall strangle you with my bare hands."

Smoke from the morning sacrifice ascends.

"Dear Ek, your voice is like an axe," his brother said.
"But what you say is true. I brought the Greeks on us.
Still, if king Menelaos kills me, as he may,
Mind this: I take no credit for my beauty.
God gives to please Himself. If He is busy—
Or asleep—one of His family may bless
A mortal soul, in my case Aphrodite.
I have been true to what she gave to me.
Not to have fallen in with Helen
Would have been free, original, and wrong."
    He stands. So debonair!
"Hail and farewell, dear Ek."

Then to the lords:

"See that the armies sit
With spears reversed and armour set aside.
Then put lord Menelaos and myself
Between you, on marked ground, and we shall fight
Until the weaker one, and so the wrong, lies dead.
    Then, having retained or repossessed her, lawfully,
Let her surviving husband lead the beauty of the world,
And what is hers, away.
    As for yourselves: you shall, before we fight,

Baptize your truce with sacrificial blood,
And pray that you may keep the words you give,
No matter who shall live. Then part,
Troy to its precincts and its provinces,
And Panachea in her troopships home
Across the sea to the belovèd land
Of Greece, of handsome wives."

Eight o'clock sun. Some movement on the Wall.

They hated him. He was exceptionally beautiful.

Clouds.

Unanswerable magnificence.

"Hear me as well," lord Menelaos says.
"One person always comes off worst.
For ten years, me. Never mind that. Though Paris started it
Everyone here has suffered for my sake.
But now that you have left the war to us
It does not matter which one dies,
Provided, when he has, you part
And ponder on it as you go your ways.
    One other thing. Though I have tried
I cannot bring myself to trust Troy's young.
Therefore, old as he is, and ailing as he is,
I ask for *Priam*! Laomedon's son,
Great King of Troy, the Lord of Ilium,
To come down here onto the plain.
That done, bring lambs—a black for Greece, a white for Troy.
Then, watched by us all, old Priam shall
Cut their young throats, and offer Heaven their blood,
For only he is King enough to make

Certain that Ilium keeps what Ilium gives,
And only he, the Lord of Holy Troy,
Adding his voice to ours, can turn those words
Into an oath so absolute
The Lord our God may bless it with His own."

Agreed.

Now dark, now bright, now watch—
As aircrews watch tsunamis send
Ripples across the Iwo Jima Deep,
Or as a schoolgirl makes her velveteen
Go dark, go bright—
The armies as they strip, and lay their bronze
And let their horses cool their hooves
Along the opposing slopes.

Agreed.

But not in Heaven.

Queen Hera: "Well?"
Athene:
    "They are about to swear and sacrifice."
    "So . . ."
Touching the left-hand corner of her mouth
    ". . . they do it frequently." And now the right.
    "A common sacrifice."
Glass down.
    "You mean, together? Greece and Troy? As one?"
    "As one."
Settling her loose-bead bodice. Turning round:

"Who to?"
"To Him."
"What for?"
"For peace."
"*Peace*—after the way that Trojan treated us?"
"Peace, home, friendship, stuff like that."
"It must be stopped."
"At once."
"It will." And so,
With faces like N O E N T R Y signs they hurried through the clouds.

Snow on Mount Ida. With Menelaos' wish
Lord Thoal and Chylabborak's son, Kykeon, walk towards Troy.

Troy. Less light. A sweetwood roof.
Sunshine through muslin. Six white feet,
Two sandalled and four bare.

They exit to the passages.

Troy. The atelier. Stitch-frames and large warp-weighted looms
". . . Paris is hated . . ."
Right-angled to the sills
". . . and so is she . . ."

The passages. Approaching feet. The women hesitate.

"Ah . . . lady . . ." Soos (smiling) says and bows
Helen, her maids, on by.
"I see young Nain has fained.
Make sure he joins us on the terraces, Pagif."

An inner court.
Gold loops across the sluiced coclackia.

"All stand."

We do.

She sits.
She lifts her veil.
She backs her needle out.
"This is the only time she stops
Thinking of how she looks . . ."

The terraces. Their awnings set since Dawn
Stepped dripping from the sea.
                    And up and in
Between the parapet, the flaps,
Murmuring shimmers drift.

Soos:
"Neomab has the plan, Pagif will check the seating,
Nain can watch. King Priam's brothers first. Pagif?"
"On the back row—"
"The *highest* row."
"—the fathers of King Priam's four full-brothers' wives;

Those brothers, and their wives; their brothers, and *their* wives."
  "Excellent."
  "Satraps of Thrace, of Bosphorus,
Marmarine Phrygiland and Hittite Anatolium Beyond . . ."

The atelier. On Helen's frame
  ". . . she will be fought for. In an hour . . ."
Achilles Reaches Troy, a nine-year work
  . . . "To death?" . . .
Whose stitchwork shows that lord
  . . . "With spears." . . .
Tall on the forepeak of a long dark ship
  . . . "Then they'll make peace." . . .
  "Poo-poo." . . .
Dismantled chariots in its waist, who has
  The kind of look that perfect health,
Astonishing, coordinated strength,
Pluperfect sight, magnificence at speed, a mind
Centred on battle, and a fearless heart
Display when found in congruence.
  . . . "What will she wear?" . . .
Observe his muscles as they move beneath his skin,
His fine, small-eared, investigative head,
His shoulder's bridge, the deep sweep of his back
Down which (plaited with Irish gold)
His never-cut redcurrant-coloured hair
Hangs in a glossy cable till its tuft
Brushes the combat-belt gripping his rump.
  What does it matter that he brought
Only 1,000 men in 20 ships?
For as they rowed their superchild between
The army's 30,000 upright oars,

"Achil! Achil! The king," the fighters cried,
"Whose godsent violence will get us home!" so loud
The local gods complained to Heaven.

"Lady . . . my lady . . . We must go,"
Cassandra, Priam's youngest girl, says as she lifts
The needle out of Helen's hand, who turns
Towards this serious 13-year-old wife—
As she once was—and lets herself be led
Across the dry-by-now coclackia, into stone.
    "There is a huge array . . . thousands of them!
And there's to be a final fight for you.
Not as per usual, though—blood everywhere.
They have calmed down, both theirs and ours,
All sitting quietly—their armour off, wheels parked,
You cannot see the foreslopes for its shine.
And round about the midday sacrifice,
Your two . . . I mean, my brother Paris and—"
    "Yes, yes."
    "Will fight to death for you below the Wall.
But first you must be viewed. You are the property.
My father's satraps want to see the property.
It is their right."

The sweetwood roof.

"Please ask if I can watch."

Cloud, like a baby's shawl.

"How many names, Pagif?"

"200 names."

"And stools?"

"200 stools."

Long rows of them. Silent and void. And suddenly

All full!

Music

An arch of bells,
A tree of china bells,
Two trees of jellyfish and cowslip bells,
All shaken soft, all shaken slow,
Backed by Egyptian clarinets.

And they pass by.

Then quadraphonic ox-horns hit their note,
And as it swims across the plain
Ten Trojan queens
Led by son-bearing Hecuba
Enter
And sit.

A lull.

And then,
And then again, but with a higher note, that note
Instantly answered by a roar of silk
As Asia stands for Laomedon's son,
Priam of Troy, the Lord of Ilium,
His litter shouldered high, lord Raphno walking by its couch,
Onto the Skean terracing.

Helen, her maids—Cumin and Tu—wait   off.

Nothing will happen till he nods.

He nods.

Below,
Chylabborak tumbles the lots.
Diomed takes one.
Paris'.
Paris will have first throw.

"We knew it was a fatal day," Tu said,
"Long before Soos announced:
'Now see the beauty to be fought for with long spears'
And Nain said Go, and up we went,
The sweat was running down between my breasts.
But then we reached the top.   And lo!
The sun stood upright in the sky, and from beneath
The murmuring glitter of the plain."

What is that noise?

The fountains?

No, my friend—it is Creation, whistling . . .

Silence and light. Beneath a mile of air
The plain is absolutely still.

Then 50,000 faces turn and tilt,
And from the tints of sand to those of sight
The colour of the plain;
And Fate, called love, possessed them.
Parting their lips, stressing each syllable,
As one the thousands said:

"Ou nem'me'sis . . ."

"Ou nem'me'sis . . ."

This boy who came from Corinth
Where the water was like wine:

"Ou nem'me'sis . . ."

This man from Abigozor on the Bosphorus;
And this unlucky nobody from Gla.

"At first, as we descended," Cumin said,
"The silence held. But as she walked across
The level leading to the lower flight
One of our earth's great leaders gasped, and stood,
And then another stood, and then the rest
Casting their gasps before her feet
As would the world its hats before a god.
    Of course, they were too old to fight,
But they were brilliant speakers.
Leaning together as they sat, they said:
'You cannot blame the world for fighting over her.'
    'There is no answer to a miracle.'
    'But she must go—
If only for our wives' and children's sake.'"

    Below,
Idomeneo carries round the winning lot.

"Sit here," Soos said—between lord Raphno and the King.
Who spat into his bowl, then took her hand and said:
    "I had a wretched night, my dear.
You lose a husband. I may lose my eldest son.
Not that I blame you, child. You were godsent.
Your people are incredible. Look there—"
    (Idomeneo)

"Tell Raphno who he is."
     She turns to him,
     "Once, though"—taking her back—"I could have pushed you all
Into the sea with my bare hands, but now—
Feel this"—his thigh—"lolly-stick wood."
     Leaving her hand there, Helen says:
     "Of all the men I know
You are the only one I would call great,
Great, and still handsome, King of Fountained Troy."
Her voice is like a scent. To keep its prick
You must, as Raphno does, lean in.

     "I need forgiveness, too.
Not that I am the kind of she who calls the priest
Each time she has a cold.
I always wanted my marriage to be perfect.
To be his. Just his. As his land is his.
And that is what my father wanted, too.
As did the world. And they are right. Quite right.
But then this thing. Your son.
I do not want to give that man a single thought.
He will not apologize. He says
A higher power gave me to him."

     "It did, my child. It did."

     "I was destroyed. The world turned upside down.
Easy to say that he has ruined my marriage
But it takes two. Put on by Love. World war. For me.
I know I have no saving touch of ugliness.
What fortune do I have? Poor Menelaos. He hid his grief.
I trust very few people now. Hector, of course.
I know it would be better if I killed myself.
But all I do is cry. And that is so annoying.
Now let me do as you have asked."

She stands. She looks. A pause. Then:

"You see that Greek with the green umbrella?
That is lord Ajax, king of Salamis. High as a man and a half.
You like it when he comes into your room,
His big, broad face, his slightly bulging, slightly shyish eyes
Make you feel safe. A pious soul,
Concerned with the opinion of his fighters,
Not above asking them to pray for him,
And such a fighter! Even Achilles
Sees Ajax as the spear Greece counts on.
    Notice the lord just coming up to him.
He is an Islander, Nyro of Simi.
A distant relative of Agamemnon,
Well born, well bred, bearing a celebrated name.
No Greek—except Achilles—can match Nyro's looks.
The trouble with him is, he cannot fight
To save his own, let alone someone else's life,
So though his father gave him three pine ships
No one would follow him to Troy
Until lord Ajax filled them.
    The man now carrying around the winner's lot
Is called Idomeneo, king of Crete.
Slack fighting niggles him, but if he lacks
The noble heart of my dear Menelaos,
My brothers say he has a valiant carelessness:
When all seems lost, there Ido is,
Grinning among the blades, inflicting big-lipped wounds,
Keeping his host's hearts high while thrusting them,
And holding them, against the enemy.

"And now," crossing to him, "for you, lord Thoal."
My how they stare. My how they wish that they were him.
Then thank God they are not.
    "Like a white leopard," Beauty said,

111

"The first thing that you sense in Thoal is,
Not strength, impressive though his is, but prudence.
Lord Thoal knows that people love to have a side,
Taking a side as simply as they take a god;
And he would like to find a god
Who tapped his foot while those who loved him danced.
He will get home. That is to say, regain his ilex napped
Snowcragbackfastnesses of Macedon.
Ithaca is his uncle. His mother, Goo'io,
Was my belovèd mother's intimate. 'Dear Goo'io,'
My mother said, 'she was so douce, so funny,
The whole world wanted her to be its wife.'
Lord Maha got her—although many said,
Beneath the trembling leaves of Mount Neritos—
What woman has not dreamed of it?—
God had her first.
    The river Styxt flows east through Macedon,
And through the Styxt, but west, the Lethe flows.
So still their voice, so smooth their interface,
Lethe like oil, Styxt almost ice,
And through their reeds you glimpse no further shore.
    Sometimes I think I am in bed at home,
And as they did, my brothers come, and pull my covers off,
And I wake up to find that Troy is nothing but a dream.
Why are they not down there?
Why have they never asked for me?"
    But Troy was not a dream, and they lay dead,
Killed by their neighbours in a hillside war,
Beneath the sheep that graze on Sparta.

    Soos coughs.
Cumin and Tu lead her away.
    Lord Thoal says:

"Favours from God to you, Priam of Asia,
And may the smile He uses to calm storms
Protect our truce.

When wrong is done, one person always suffers most.
For Greece, lord Menelaos is that one.
He knows that Paris, your good-looking son,
Began, and has continued in this wrong,
But also knows that everyone,
Not least yourself, has suffered for it.

Therefore, to make as sure as sure can be
That this day is the last day of our war,
Lord Menelaos asks that you, Great Sir,
Come down onto the plain with us,
And sacrifice with us,
For you alone are King enough to make
Certain that Ilium keeps what Ilium gives,
And can alone, as Lord of Holy Troy,
Promote those words into an oath, so absolute,
Our Father, God, may bless it with His voice."

The windmills on the Wall are still.
King Priam stands. Then lifts his withered arms, and says:

"To the plain."

And on the plain the drums begin to beat.

White horses on the sea, and on the shore,
Where the passing of the days is the only journey,
    See
The first of the Immortals, known as God,
Strolling along the sand.

Suddenly Lord Poseidon puts his head above the waves:

"Good morning."
"And to you."

A pause. And then:

"Could I have Your opinion of the wall?"
"The Wall?"
"The new, Greek wall."
"You mean their palisade."
"I mean their wall."
"They have begun a palisade, but not a wall.
Walls, as you know, are made of stone," God said,
As He resumed His steps.
    "And as *You* know," his brother said (wading along),
"We split the world in two.
You got the sky. I got the sea. And the earth—
Especially what the humans call the shore—
Was common ground. Correct?"
    "Correct."
    "Then why is Greece allowed to build a wall
Across my favourite bay with nothing said?
Did I hear aves? No. Pae'ans? Not one.
Pfwah . . . do what you like with Lord Poseidon's honey sand,
No need to sacrifice a shrimp to *him*.
Just up she goes! Renowned as far as light can see!
The god—some seaside lizard sneezing in the weed.
His dignity—a rag. A common rag."

    "Brother," God said, "your altars smoke on every coast,
To catch your voice, grave saints in oilskins lean across the waves.
Try not to let the humans bother you—
My full associate in destiny. Between ourselves"

(Leading him out onto the sand) "I may wind up this war,
And then, Pope of the Oceans, with Greece rowing home
You will have sacrifices up to here . . .
And as they heave, your train of overhanging crests
Obliterates their spade-and-bucket Maginot Line.
But later—when I give the nod."

Hardly are those words out, when:

"Rubbish!"

They hear, and looking round they see
(Steadying her red-sepal hat with the russet-silk flutes)
Creamy-armed Hera with teenage Athene
(Holding their scallop-edged parasol high)
As they wobble their way down the dunes,
Shouting:

". . . truce . . ."
". . . and an oath . . ."
"For peace . . ."
". . . dirty peace."
"In Your name . . ."

But as they near their voices fall,
And as they slow their eyes fall, too,
For looking into His when He is cross
Is like running into searchlights turned full on.

"Imparadise Mount Ida, and," God said,
"Tell Heaven to meet me there,"
Then He was gone. And Lord Poseidon, gone
Backward into the depths,
His tower of bubbles reaching to the light.

Fierce chrome. Weapon-grade chrome
Trembling above the slopes.
And standing in it, leaning on their spears, among their wheels,
The enemies. And over all,
The city's altars, smoking.

A messenger runs between the lines.

Then nothing.

Then a boy selling water.

Then nothing.

Then nothing.

"Come on! Come *on!*"

Then 50 kings walk through

And greet—

Dressed in a silver-wool pelisse, his crown
Of separate leaves (of separate shades of gold)
Each representing one of Ilium's trees—
As he steps from his car onto the plain,
Priam of Troy. Who says:

"Paramount Agamemnon, from my Temple font
Accept this pyx of consecrated fire,"
(That Soos holds out),
"Ilium's eternal promise to our Lord
That Troy shall keep the word it gives,

That when your brother, or my son, lies dead,
Our war will end."

   "*Ave!*"

That is:

   "*Ave!*"

   As Thoal and Kykeon slip
Into the line among the younger best
   "*Ave!*"
A lordly pace behind these lordly men
As they process between the slopes,
As they process, carrying the black lamb and the white,
King Agamemnon and Prince Hector, both,
Behind Dynastic Priam (8'6"),
Correctly known as the Great King of Troy,
Himself behind a boy, who gives, each second step,
A rim-shot on his drum.

   In a plain bowl
Soos and Talthibios mix
Water and wine
Then pour it over Hector's spear-arm hand,
   "*Ave!*" (but soft—some, trembling)
Then pour
   "*Ave!*" (so soft—some, weeping)
It over Agamemnon's spear-arm hand.
Then these are dried.
Then Hector takes King Agamemnon's knife
(His feasting knife) and crops a tuft
Of lovely, oily wool from each lamb's nape.
   And when these fingerfuls

(By Akafact for Troy, for Greece Antilochos)
Were taken to the overlords
And each had kept a hair and passed the curl along,
King Agamemnon said:

"Your terms are granted, Troy.
The woman will be fought for, now, to death.
Paris shall have first throw."

It is the moment for the prayer.

"My son?"

Prince Hector says:

"God of All Gods, Most Holy and Most High,
Imperial Lord of Earth, Sire of the Night,
And of the Rising Stars of Night, true King
Of waste and wall, and of our faithful selves,
We ask You from our hearts to let us end
Through one just death our memorable war."

This was Prince Hector's prayer,
Tenderly, softly prayed.
    And as the silence that came after it
Increased the depth and wonder of the day,
The heroes filled their drinking cups with wine
Sainted with water, which is best, and sipped;
And what in them was noble, grew;
And truthfulness, with many meanings, spread
Over the slopes and through the leafy spears
As Priam thrust the knife into the white lamb's throat
(Which did not struggle very much) and pressed it down,
Into the black lamb's throat, and pressed it down;
Then, as the overlords spilt out their cups,

Lifted the pan of blood Talthibios had caught,
Bright red in silver to the sun.

"*Amen.*"

And then:

—Two
        —Two
                —Two-three

The drum.

"*Amen . . .*" (but stronger now) and now
The shin and bodice bronze of those about to fight
    —"Yes!"—
    —"Yes!"—
Is carried up and down the measured ground.

The lords:

"We swear to kill, and then castrate, whoever breaks the oath."

And as the spears, the cymbal shields, the freshly gilded crests,
    —"Yes!"—
    —"Yes!"—
Are carried round,
The lords:

"*Let both be brave, dear God. Dear God,
See that the one who caused this war shall die.*"

Silence again. Then from the blue
A long low roll of thunder, of the kind—
And then again, again—that bears fat drops.

Though no drops came.
    Finally, though, the sky stopped muttering. And then,
100,000 palms rose with their voices, and:

"To You!"
"To You!"

Billowed into the light.

Here comes a hand

That banks

Topples through sunlit music
Into a smoothdownsideways roll

Then

Hovers above Ida imparadised

Salutes the gods, and

Out.

    But they just smile. They are the gods.
They have all the time in the world.
And Lord Apollo orchestrates their dance,
And Leto smiles to see her son, the son of God,
Playing his lyre among them, stepping high,
Hearing his Nine sing how the gods have everlasting joy,
Feasting together, sleeping together,
Kind, color, calendar no bar, time out of mind,
And how we humans suffer at their hands,

Childish believers, fooled by science and art,
Bound for Oblivion—
Until

T R U M P E T S !

S U S T A I N E D !

Sustained by sunlit chords:

"High King of Heaven, Whose temple is the sky,"

Now the Nine sing, as,
Led by a flock of children through the dance,
God comes, lofty and calm, and lifts His hand.

Then in the hush, but far and clear, all Heaven heard:

"To You!"
"To You!"

"To You!"
"To You!"

The measured ground.

In a fast slouch, the Trojan lord,
With a belligerent snarl, the Greek,
Come on to it.
Both men stand tall. Both men look large.
And though the Trojans hate him, they are proud of him,
Paris, his mirror bronze, his hair:
"Be brave!"

But heroes are not frightened by appearances.
Under his breath lord Menelaos says:
"I hate that man. I am going to kill that man.
I want to mark his face. I want to shout into his face:
You are dead. You are no longer in this world."

The drum.

The 50 feet between them. Then:

"Begin."

The Trojan turns.

Five steps.

Re-turns, and right arm back, runs
—Four   —three   —two
And airs his point for Menelaos' throat.

But heroes are not worried by such sights.
Even as he admired the skill with which
Paris released his spear *"Dear God"* lord Menelaos prayed
"Stand by me" as he watched the bronze head lift
"Think of the oxen I" then level out *"have killed for You"*
And float towards his face. And only then
(As when, modelling a skirt, if childbride Helen asked:
"Yes?" he would cock his head) he cocked his head
And let the spear cruise by.
   And

—"Yes!"—

Cried the Greeks, but by that time
Their hero has done more than hurl his own, and

—"Yes!"—

He is running under it, as fast as it, and

—"Yes!"—

As the 18-inch head hits fair Paris' shield
And knocks him backwards through the air
(Bent like a gangster in his barber's chair)
Then thrusts on through that round
And pins it, plus his sword arm, to the sand
The Greek is over him, sword high, and screaming:

"Now you believe me! Now you understand me!"

Smashing the edge down *right, left, right,*
On either side of Paris' face, and:

"That's the stuff! That's the stuff! Pretty to watch!"

Queen Hera and Athene shout, as Paris' mask
Goes *left*, goes *right,* and from the mass:

"Off with his cock! Off with his cock!" *right-left,*

And on the Wall: "God kill him," (Helen to herself),
As Menelaos, happy now, raises his sword
To give the finishing stroke, and—cheering, cheering, cheering—
Down it comes: and shatters on Lord Paris' mask.

No problem!

A hundred of us pitch our swords to him . . .
Yet even as they flew, their blades
Changed into wings, their pommels into heads,

Their hilts to feathered chests, and what were swords
Were turned to doves, a swirl of doves,
And waltzing out of it, in oyster silk,
Running her tongue around her strawberry lips
While repositioning a spaghetti shoulder-strap,
The Queen of Love, Our Lady Aphrodite,
Touching the massive Greek aside with one
Pink fingertip, and with her other hand
Lifting Lord Paris up, big as he was,
In his bronze bodice heavy as he was,
Lacing his fingers with her own, then leading him,
Hidden in wings, away.

Then both slopes looked this way and that and then around,
For there was no one who would hide that man.
And Menelaos is in torment, yes,
Is running naked up and down
Saying things like: "Where did he go?"
"Somebody must have seen him go?" and then
He has gone down on both his knees, naked, on both his knees,
Shaking his fists at Heaven, and shouting out:

"God God—Meek, Time-Free Trash,
Your hospitality is mocked.
And so are You. And so is Greece. And so am I."

Athene comes to God.

"Signor?"
"Chou-Chou . . . how nice . . .
Congratulations on your victory."
"My what?"
"A clear, decisive victory for your Greeks.

124

So that is that. Their champion she goes home,
The Sea can scrub that palisade, and peace can go the rounds."

The armies wait.

Picking a cotton from his sleeve: "Pa-pa," Athene said,
"This is not fairyland. The Trojans swore an oath
To which You put Your voice."
    "I did not."
"Father, You did. All Heaven heard You. Ask the Sea."
"I definitely did not."
"Did-did-did-did—and no returns."

The armies wait.

"Dearest Pa-pa, the oath said one should die.
The Trojan was about to die. He did not die.
Nobody died. Therefore the oath is dead.
Killed by a Trojan. Therefore Troy goes down."

Drivers conducting underbody maintenance.

"Father, You must act.
Side with the Trojans, Greece will say,
Were we fools to believe in His thunder?
Why serve a God who will not serve His own?"

And giving her a kiss, He said:

"Child, I am God,
Please do not bother me with practicalities."

Hector and Agamemnon. Slope sees slope.
Such heat!

King Agamemnon says:
"Outstanding Prince, we live in miracles.
Our Lord and God, Whose voice dethrones the hills,
Has seen the woman won. Therefore I say,
Let her first husband have her, and her gold.
If not, I shall fill Troy with fire
And give its sobbings to the wind."

Still heat.
The Gate, all eyes.

Hector:

"Enemy King, your brother, Menelaos,
Shall lead his wife, and that wife's gold, away.
And while she says goodbye, and Wall and plain
Wait till she walks across the sand into her husband's arms,
Let us, who fought for her together,
Make shade, and sit, and eat together,
Then listen to our story and shed tears
Together, for our dead, and for ourselves,
Among our horses and our hosts before we part,
You in your ships to your belovèd land,
We to our open city, or Beyond,
This afternoon, the favourable, on which,
In answer to my prayer, our rest began."

Rain over Europe.
Queen Hera puts her hate-filled face around its fall
And says to God:

"I want Troy dead.
Its swimming pools and cellars filled with limbs,

Its race, rotten beneath the rubble, oozing pus,
Even at noon the Dardanelles lit up,
All that is left a bloodstain by the sea."
     "Hold on . . ."
     "Shut up, you whelk."
     "Silence you both."
     "No, no," (wagging a finger in His face)
"I shall not stop. You shall not make me stop.
Troy asks for peace? Troy shall have peace. The peace of the dead—
Or You will have no peace until it does."

     The terraces.
Teethee, her granny-slave, calls Helen with her head.

     "Athena?"

     Sniff.

     God sighs and says:

     "Magnificas,
You know how fond I am of Troy.
Its humans have acknowledged Me, and prayed to Me,
And raised high smoke to Me for centuries.
If I agree to your destroying it
And them, you must allow Me to destroy
Three Greek cities whose ratepayers have
Been faithful to yourselves as Troy to Me,
And when I do, remembering Troy, you will not say a word."

     Their heads go close.

     Below,
Cattle are being chosen for the feast.

127

Athene: "We accept.
Person for person, wall for wall,
Mycenae, Corinth, Sparta, match Troy's worth,
And they have prayed to us, etcetera,
For just as long as Ilus and his offspring have to You.
Let us kill Troy—do what You like with them."
    "I can be comfortable with that," God said.
"Have the Nine sing again."

    "Dear Shepherd of the Clouds," His sister said,
"I hate these quarrels just as much as You.
Send 'Thene to the plain, and while she finds
A Trojan fame-seeker to get the war
Back on the boil, and everything to normal,
Please be the god who is a God to me."

    But He had something more to say.
He stands: the Lord and Master of the Widespread Sky:

    "After today,
On pain of being thrown into the void
To drift alive, alone,
From universe to universe for all eternity,
The plain is closed to Heaven—including both of you."
    Cloud coral in deep seas. People with cameras.
Those sunlit chords.
    "So child," (now smiling at Athene) "do
As my wifely sister says." And she
Cast herself earthwards with a shriek of joy
That echoed back as: "I know just the man!"

    Note Pandar's facts:
Sired by lord Kydap of the Hellespont,

128

Competitive, north Ilium's star archer,
He likes to chat, but has a problem keeping off himself.
And now, as Hector says: "Make shade . . ." we centre him,
Practising bowpulls, running on the spot,
Surrounded by the shields he led to Troy.
                              But O,
As Hector reached ". . . our rest began . . ." a gleam
(As when Bikini flashlit the Pacific)
Staggered the Ilian sky, and by its white
Each army saw the other's china face, and cried:
    "O please!"
(As California when tremors rise)
    "O please!"
As through it came a brighter, bluer light
Gliding, that then seemed like a pair of lips
Hovering, and then a kiss, a nursing kiss
On Pandar's wide-eyed mouth, who closed his lids
And sipped its breath, and thus became
The dreaded teenaged god, Athene's, host.

Pandar has never felt so confident. So *right*.
His bow-slave, Deedam, massages his neck.
    "De-de, I am a man.
Like day is light is how I am a man.
But am I man enough, I ask myself,
To put a shot through Menelaos' neck,
While he is out there waiting for his wife?"
    "He is our enemy. Our duty is to kill him, sir."
    "And their cause with him, De-de. Think of that."
    "Paris would give us a south tower, sir."
    "Appropriate for a winning shot."
    "An unforgettable shot."
Horses are being watered. Fires lit.

Such heat!
　　"However, De-de, one thing is against it."
　　"Sir?"
　　"With their cause gone, the Greeks will sail,
So I shall lose my chance to kill Achilles."
　　"In that case, sir—"
　　"No, De-de, Troy comes first."
He stands.
　　"I have decided. I will shoot him now.
Prepare the Oriental bow, and I will pray."

The sweetwood roof.

　　"Until I closed our doorbolt," Cumin said,
"Old Teethee nattered about Paris' charm, his smile, etc.
Then all at once her squeaky words became
Spacious and clear.
　　I sensed we were in trouble. Tu was green. At the same time
I wanted to be kissed and licked all over.
This is how Aphrodité sounds when she commands our flesh
I told myself. And I was right. So we were lost. But then
Twice in one day my lady was my lord.
　　Putting her beautiful world-famous face
Down into Teethee's crumpled face, Greek Helen said:
　　'I know your voice, lewd Queen. By using me
　　You aim to stymie lake-eyed Hera's spite.'—
Talking poor Teethee backwards round the floor—
　　'So by a crossroads or a lake, a cave,
　　Only this morning catwalked for the son
　　Of some Nyanzan cattle king whose Yes! to you
　　Has accessed him to me. Tu, Cumin—pack.
　　Make sure my pubic jewellery is on top.

130

Yours, too. God only knows whose threesome we shall be.'—
Teethee now edging sideways down the wall.—
    'And all because the winner wants me back.
Lord Menelaos wants me back.
Oh yes he does. Oh yes he bloody does.
So your Judge Paris kisses me goodbye.
        Well, that's soon fixed
As you and he have such a meaningful relationship
Take my place. Of *course* you will give up your immortality:
Paradise dumped for love! Become a she—
How do I look? Will high heels help? And if,
If you try hard, your best, he may—note *may*—
Promote your exdivinity *Wife*. The apogee
Of standard amenities. No. That is wrong. I take that back.
Before the end of your productive life you bear
"A *boy?*"
"*Unfortunately not . . .*"
Why did you make me leave my land? My child?
Look at me. All of you. My head is full of pain.
Ih!—there it goes. Pepper my breasts.
Why should I go to Paris. I am lost.'
    Those were her words. And as the last of them
Fell from her downcast face, Teethee reached up
And with her fingers closed those vivid lips."

    Then in that handsome room, in Troy, it was
Just as it is for us when Solti's stick comes down
And a wall of singers hits their opening note
And the hair on the back of your neck stands up.
As she pulled Helen down, her form rose up
But not as Teethee's form, nor as Miss Must
Wringing her hair out, wet. But as she is:
A god. As Aphrodité, Queen of Love, her breasts
Alert and laden with desire in their own light,

131

Gloss of a newly-opened chestnut burr, her hair,
Her feet in sparkling clogs, her voice:
   "Do stop this nonsense, Helen, dear.
You are not lost. You never shall be lost.
You are my representative on earth.
You look around you—and you wait.
Try not to play the thankless bitch:
'Such a mistake to leave my land, my kiddywink . . .'
What stuff. Millions would give that lot
For half the looks that I have given you.
   You there: yes, you with the Egyptian eyes,
Prepare her bath. And you, Miss Quivering, strip her."
   They do as they are told.
   "Turn round."
Impartial as a sunbeam, her regard.
   "Your sweat, your wrinkle cream—quite useful. Eh?
Go through." And as they did:
   "You wear a crown of hearts. Your duty is
To stir and charm the wonder of the world.
To raise the cry: *Beauty is so unfair!*"
Leaves. Tiles. The sky. "And so it is.
Free. And unfair. And strong. A godlike thing."
The water's net across the water's floor.
   "Be proud. You have brought harm. Tremendous boys
Of every age have slaughtered one another
Just for you!" Tu works the loofah down her spine,
"And as God knows no entertainment quite
So satisfying as war, your name has crossed His lips . . ."
(Now in a chair with one clog dangling.)
"Think of it, Elly—crossed His lips. And one fine day
The richest city in the world will burn for you,
Lie on its side and cry into the sand for you—
But, Sweetie, do not be too quick to leave.
After that business with the palisade
The Sea will see no Greek worth mentioning gets home.

132

"Dry her."
We did.
"Oil her."
We did.
"Dust her with gold.

"Come here."
Tall, dignified, alone,
Wearing a long, translucent, high-necked dress.
Gold beads the size of ant-heads separate her girdle's pearls.
   "Bear this in mind:
Without my love, somewhere between the Greek and Trojan lines
A cloud of stones would turn your face to froth.
So, when they lift the curtains, and he looks—you hesitate.
And then you say: Take me, and I shall please you."
   Pause.
"What do you say?"
"Take me, and I shall please you."
"Good. Now in you go."

Lord Pandar prays:

"Dear Lord of Archers and Dear Lady Lord,
Bare-breasted Artemis of Shots and Snares,
My blessings to you both
For blessing me with perfect sight
And for the opportunity to shoot
The Greek who caused this war,
A man scarce worthy to be killed
By me, your gifted worshipper."

While his grey bow-slave slips the bowstring's eye
Over the bow's iron ear, then plucks its string,

And hearing—as his owner stands—the proper note,
Hands him the bow, and bows. Then stands well back
Watching his blameless fame-seeker assume
The best position for a vital shot.

The shields divide. Lord Pandar's shoulder blades
Meet in the middle of his back; the arrow's nock
Is steady by his nostril and its head
Rests on the bosom of the bow.
Someone has passed a cup to Menelaos,
And, as his chin goes up, childe Pandar sights his throat,
Then frees the nock: and gently as the snow
Falls from an ilex leaf onto the snow
Athene left him, and the head moved out.

But the god did not forget you, Menelaos!
Even as she left, Athene tipped the shot
Down, past your brother,
—THOCK—
Into your pubic mound.

Wait for the pain, wait for the pain, and here it comes,
Wham! Wham!
    ". . . aha . . ."

Shield shade. Field surgery.
Odysseus, Ajax, Thoal, tears in their eyes,
Then Makon, Panachea's surgeon, saying: "Shears."
    ". . . aha . . ." (but soft) and,
Opening the loincloth (fishline rolled in silver)
    There it is: in past its barbs,
A wooden needle resting in red wool, that Makon clips
    ". . . aha . . ."
    Then: "This" (the vinegar) "may sting." And as it did,
Paramount Agamemnon, King of kings,

Sighed as he knelt beside you on the sand,
And all his lords sighed, too, and all his underlords
Sighed, and though as yet they knew not why, the Greeks
All sighed as Makon cut, and Agamemnon said:
"I love you, Menelaos. Do not die. Please do not die,"
(And cut) "for you are all I have.
And if you die the Greeks will sail" (and cut)
"Leaving my honour and your wife behind."
Makon has nodded, and, as Jica kneels,
He and boy Aesculapius pull ". . . aha . . ."
The quadrilateral tabs of flesh his cuts have made
Back from the head for Jica's finger-strength to hold
Back and apart while Aesculapius swabs
And Makon looks, and Agamemnon says:
"Oh, Menelaos, I have done so much
For your and Helen's sake, do not desert me now.
You know what everyone will say. *He was a fool,*
When have the Trojans ever kept their word?
He should have done what they did—only first."
Makon sits back . . . "And as the Fleet pulls out
The Trojans will parade her, and her gold,
Along the beach," the arrow-head has thrust
Into the cartilage coupling the pubic arch,
"But nobody will blame Odysseus
Although he organized the fight." And looking up
His brother said: "It may not be that bad . . ."
"It will be worse. I shall be treated like a strapless she.
Ignored. Pushed to one side." His head is in his hands.
Now for the pain: as Jica parts the arch,
Makon will use his teeth/his neck to draw
The head out of the gristle by its stump.
His face goes down. He breathes. He bites. He signs:
And smoothly as a fighter-plane peels off
". . . aha . . . aha . . ." (my God, that man takes pain,
As well as women do) lord Jica has the bones apart

135

And sweetly as he drew his mother's milk
Makon has drawn the barbed thing out
And dropped it into Aesculapius' hand,
Who looks (as he unlids the anaesthetic paste), says: "Clean."
Oh, stupid Pandar . . .

King Agamemnon stands.

His body shines. His face is terrible. His voice is like a cliff.
Taking a spear, and stepping, as his lords divide,
Out inbetween the slopes, he calls into the sky:

"Dear Lord, I know that You will not forget
The wine we poured, the lambs whose blood we shed,
And in Your own good time You will reduce
Truce-calling Troy, truce-spoiling Troy,
Oathmaking Troy, oathbreaking Troy,
Cowardly Troy, treacherous Troy to dust, to dust."

And now he takes a step, his lords behind,
Towards Hector, and he says:

"Bad Prince, God may take time. My time is now.
To shed your blood. To shed your dark red blood.
Your gleaming blood. And as you die
The last thing that you see will be my jeering face,
The last voice that you hear, my voice,
Confiding how my heroes served your wife
And kicked your toddler off the Wall."

The terraces are empty.

The speaker turns
Back to his long bronze slope of men, and roars:

"There they are!"

"There they are!"

"The traitor race!"

"Let them die now!"

Troy. They lift the curtains. Paris looks.

"You sent for me?"
"You are my wife."
"And his."

"I have offended you."

"Let's not burst into tears over that."
"I owe you flowers."
"Then go back down and fight for me again."
She has not raised her eyes.
"It will be painless. He is fast—and heavy."

"Tu."
"Lord?"
"My cloth."

Naked. His curls
Bursting around his head like sunlit frost.
His eyes—so kind.

"Your death will be the best for everyone.
Troy will reopen. I shall sail for Greece.

And you will not survive your cowardice."
"I—"
"Then go back down and fight for me again.
'I am his better. I shall take his life,' is what I heard."

His shirt. His boots.
On.
On, and—

"Cumin."
"Lady?"
"Retie my girdle."

While she does:

"I have not finished."
"Yes?"
"What happens if you kill each other?"
And through the lattice, in the pause—but far:

"N O W !"
"N O W !"

"Close it, Tu."
"My lord."
"Leave it, Tu. I want to hear the plain."
Shirt. Boots. All done.
"Well?"
He stands.
"If I had not said what I said you would have stayed,"
Turning away from him.

"N O W !"
"N O W !"

"Oh go then—you know what they say.
Up here: 'The bitch will see us sold.'
Down there: 'Leave her to Heaven.' "
   He goes towards her back.
   "I will not let you go until you say."
Cumin has closed the latticing, and now
She leads the others out.

   "Beauty," he says, "I bless the day, the month, the year,
The season and the spirits of the place
Where we two met. Such heat!
But we were shivering with lust.
And when the crew had gone ashore to sacrifice,
Me, nude on the rug, you, little big girl,
Still with one thing on: 'Shall I be naked, too?' you said,
And then: 'Watch me get rid of it!' and threw it off,
And then yourself into my arms,
Into my arms, the world all gone,
And the sun rose early to see us."

R aise your binoculars.
The dukes of Troy—Hector among them.
Hector's face. Faces near Hector's face.
Aeneas, Gray, Sarpedon, Akafact.
Faces near Hector's face say *Now*. Who says:
"When God says strike, we strike—"
   Swing to the Greeks.
See them helping each other on with their bronze,
   Aeneas: "Now."
Fastening each other's straps.
   Sarpedon: "Now."
"—but I will recognize that moment when it comes."

Yet *Now* has caught his slope. And now,
Quibuph, holding his vulture-plumed helmet,
Catches his eye. Then with his silver yard
Poised by his lips, T'lesspiax, his trumpeter,
Catches his eye. And then it is his next,
Chylabborak, adding his *Now* to theirs.

    But we are not in fairyland.
We know that it was not till God turned to His son,
The Lord of Light and Mice, and said:

    "Let Thetis have her way,"
That Hector, whose clear voice
Rose like an arrow through the trembling air,
Cried:

    "Hearts, full hearts, courageous hearts,
Our lives belong to God and Ilium!" and waved them on—
Their flutes screeching across the thunder of their feet,
Their chariots deep in plumes.

    But heroes are not frightened by appearances,
And as that bull-sea-roar of eight-foot shields came travelling on,
The Greeks shook hands and said goodbye to one another,
Briefly, because the Trojan Wall-wide:

    "N O W!"

    "N O W!"
Meant you could hardly hear a word you said.

    And when the armies met, they paused,
And then they swayed, and then they moved
Much like a forest making its way through a forest.

    And after ten years the war has scarcely begun,
And Apollo but breathes for the Greeks to be thrown
(As shingle is onto a road by the sea)
Back down the dip, swell, dip of the plain.

    And now it has passed us the sound of their war
Resembles the sound of Niagara
Heard from afar in the still of the night.

War Music

Patrocleia

Now hear this:
While they fought around the ship from Thessaly,
Patroclus came crying to the Greek.

   "Why tears, Patroclus?" Achilles said.
"Why hang about my ankles like a child
Pestering its mother, wanting to be picked up,
Expecting her to stop what she is at,
Getting its way through snivels?
   You have bad news from home?
Someone is dead, Patroclus? Your father? Mine?
But news like that is never confidential.
If such was true, you, me, and all the Myrmidons
Would cry together.
   It's the Greeks, Patroclus, isn't it?
You weep because 2,000 Greeks lie dead beside their ships.
But did you weep when those same Greeks condoned my wrongs?
If I remember rightly you said nothing."

   And Patroclus:
"Save your hate, Achilles. It will keep.
Our cause is sick enough without your grudging it my tears.
   You know Merionez is wounded?
Lord Thoal, too—his thigh: King Agamemnon, even. Yet
Still you ask: *Why tears?*
   Is there to be no end to your grudge?
No, no; don't shrug me off. Mind who it is that asks:
Not the smart Ithacan; not Agamemnon. Me.
And God forbid I share the niceness of a man
Who when his friends go down sits tight

And finds his vindication in their pain.
   They are dying, Achilles. Dying.
Think, if you cannot think of them, of those
Who will come after them; what they will say:
   Achilles the Resentful—can you hear it?
Achilles, strong? . . . *The Strongest of the Strong*—and just as well
Seeing his sense of wrong became so heavy.
   Shameful that I can talk to you this way."
   All still.
   "Let me go out and help the Greeks, Achilles.
Let me command your troops. Part of them, then?
And let me wear your bronze."
   Still.
   "Man—it will be enough!
Me, dressed as you, pointing the Myrmidons . . .
The sight alone will make Troy pause, and say:
'It's him.' A second look will check them, turn them,
Give the Greeks a rest (although war has no rest) and turned,
Nothing will stop us till they squat behind their Wall."

   And so he begged for death.

   "Why not add Agamemnon to your argument?" Achilles said.
"King vain, King fretful, greedy Agamemnon,
Eager to eat tomorrow's fame today.
   Go on . . . 'He was a sick man at the time, Achilles.
He did it to avoid unpleasantness, Achilles.
Achilles, he was not too well advised.'"
   Staring each other down until he said:
   "O love
I am so glutted with resentment that I ache.
   Tell me, have I got it wrong?
Didn't he take the girl I won?—
Didn't his widow lords agree
That she was mine by right of rape and conquest? Yet

146

When it comes to it, they side with him:
The King who robs the man on whom his crown depends.
   Yet done is done; I cannot grudge forever.
Take what you want: men, armour, cars, the lot."
   Easy to see his loss was on the run
Him standing, saying:
   "Muster our Myrmidons and thrust them, hard,
Just here"—marking the sand—"between the enemy
And the Fleet.
   Aie! . . . they are impudent, these Trojans . . .
They stroke our ships,
Fondle their slim black necks, and split them, yes—
Agamemnon's itchy digits make me absent,
My absence makes them brave, and so, Patroclus,
Dear Agamemnon's grab-all/lose-all flows.
   All right: if not Achilles, then his vicar.
Forget the spear. Take this"—one half its length—"instead.
You say Merionez is out? Bad. Bad. And Ajax, too? Far worse.
No wonder all I hear is
Hector, Hector, Hector, everywhere Hector,
As if he were a god split into 60.
   Hurry, Patroclus, or they will burn us out . . .
But listen first. Hard listening? Good.
   Hear what I want:
My rights, and my apologies. No less.
And that is all.
As for his gifts . . . well, if he deserves a favour,
We shall see.
   One other thing before you go:
Don't overreach yourself, Patroclus.
Without me you are something, but not much.
Let Hector be. He's mine—God willing.
In any case he'd make a meal of you,
And I don't want you killed.
But neither do I want to see you shine at my expense.

147

So mark my word:
No matter how, how much, how often, or how easily you win,
Once you have forced the Trojans back, you stop.
    There is a certain brightness in the air:
It means the Lord Apollo is too close
For you to disobey me and be safe.
    You know Apollo loves the Trojans; and you know
That even God, our Father, hesitates
To block the Lord of Light.
    O friend,
I would be glad if all the Greeks lay dead
While you and I demolished Troy alone."

Cut to the Fleet:
Then to the strip between the rampart and the ditch.

    The air near Ajax was so thick with arrows, that,
As they came, their shanks tickered against each other;
And under them the Trojans swarmed so thick
Ajax outspread his arms, turned his spear flat,
And simply *pushed.* Yet they came clamouring back until
So many Trojans had a go at him
The iron chaps of Ajax' helmet slapped his cheeks
To soft red pulp, and his head reached back and forth
Like a clapper inside a bell made out of sword blades.
    Maybe, even with no breath left,
Big Ajax might have stood it yet; yet
Big and all as he was, Prince Hector meant to burn that ship:
And God was pleased to let him.

    Pulling the Trojans back a yard or two
He baited Ajax with his throat; and Ajax took.

As the spear lifted, Hector skipped in range;
As Ajax readied, Hector bared his throat again;
And, as Ajax lunged, Prince Hector jived on his right heel
And snicked the haft clean through its neck
Pruning the bronze nose off—Aie!—it was good to watch
Big Ajax and his spear blundering about for, O,
Two seconds went before he noticed it had gone.
    But when he noticed it he knew
God stood by Hector's elbow, not by his;
That God was pleased with Hector, not with Ajax;
And, sensibly enough, he fled.

The ship was burned.

October.
The hungry province grows restive.
The Imperial army must visit the frontier.
Dawn.
The captains arrive behind standards;
A tiger's face carved on each lance-butt.
And equipment for a long campaign
Is issued to every soldier.
First light.
Men stand behind the level feathers of their breath.
A messenger runs from the pearl-fringed tent.
The captains form a ring. They read.
The eldest one points north. The others nod.

Likewise his heroes stood around Achilles: listening.
And the Myrmidons began to arm and tramp about the beach.
First sunlight off the sea like thousands of white birds.
    Salt haze.

149

Imagine wolves: an hour ago the pack
Hustled a stag, then tore it into shreds.
Now they have gorged upon its haunch
They need a drink to wash their curry down.
So, sniffing out a pool, they loll their long,
Thin, sharp-pointed tongues therein; and as they lap
Rose-coloured billows idle off their chops,
Drifting throughout the water like pink smoke.

Likewise his Myrmidons,
Their five commanders on his right,
Patroclus on his left,
And the onshore wind behind Achilles' voice:

"Excellent killers of men!
Today Patroclus leads; and by tonight,
You, behind him, will clear the Trojans from our ditch.
And who at twilight fails to bring
At least one Trojan head to deck
The palings of our camp can sleep outside
With Agamemnon's lot."

The columns tightened.
The rim of each man's shield
Overlapped the face of his neighbour's shield
Like clinkered hulls—as shipwrights call them when they lay
Strake over strake, caulked against seas.
As they moved off, the columns tightened more;
Until, to one above, it seemed, five wide black straps
Studded with bolts were being drawn across the sand.

Before Achilles sailed to Troy
His women packed and put aboard his ship

A painted oak box filled with winter clothes;
Rugs for his feet, a fleece-lined windcheater—
You know the sort of thing. And in this box
He kept an eye-bowl made from ivory and horn
Which he, and only he, used for communion.
    When he had spoken to his troops he took it out,
Rubbed sulphur crystals on its inner face
Then washed and dried his hands, before,
Spring water rinsed, brimming with altar-wine,
He held it at arm's length, and prayed:

"Our Father, Who rules in Heaven,
Because Your will is done where will may be
Grant me this prayer
As You have granted other prayers of mine:
Give my Patroclus Your victory;
Let him show Hector he can win
Without me at his side;
And grant, above all else, O Lord,
That when the Trojans are defeated, he
Returns to me unharmed."

God heard his prayer and granted half of it.
Patroclus would rout the Trojans; yes:
But not a word was said about his safe return.
No, my Achilles, God promised nothing of the kind,
As carefully you dried your cup,
As carefully replaced it in its box,
Then stood outside your gate and watched
Your men and your Patroclus go by.

Hornets occasionally nest near roads.
In the late spring they breed, feeding their grubs

151

And feeding off the tacky sweat those grubs exude.
Ignorant children sometimes poke
Sticks into such a nest, and stir. The hornets swarm.
Often a swollen child dies that night.
Sometimes they menace passers-by instead.

No such mistake today.

Swarming up and off the beach
Patroclus swung the Myrmidons left at the ditch.
    Keeping it on their right they streamed
Along the camp's main track; one side, the battered palisade;
On the other, ships.
    Things were so close you could not see your front;
And from the footplate of his wheels, Patroclus cried:
    "For Achilles!"
As the enemies closed.

    The Trojans lay across the ship
Most of them busy seeing that it burned.
Others slid underneath and were so occupied
Knocking away the chocks that kept it upright
They did not see Patroclus stoop.
But those above did.
    In less time than it takes to dip and light a match
Achilles' helmet loomed above their cheeks
With Myrmidons splayed out on either side
Like iron wings.
    Dropping the pitch
They reached for javelins, keelspikes, boat-hooks, O,
Anything to keep Achilles off—
Have he and Agamemnon patched things up?

    Patroclus aimed his spear where they were thickest.
That is to say,

Around the chariot commander, Akafact.
   But as Patroclus threw
The ship's mast flamed from stem to peak and fell
Lengthwise across the incident.
   Its fat waist clubbed the hull's top deck
And the ship flopped sideways.
   Those underneath got crunched
And howling Greeks ran up
To pike the others as they slithered off.
   This fate was not for Akafact:
Because the mast's peak hit the sand no more than six
Feet from Patroclus' car, the horses shied,
Spoiling his cast. Nothing was lost.
   As Akafact fell back, back arched,
God blew the javelin straight; and thus
Mid-air, the cold bronze apex sank
Between his teeth and tongue, parted his brain,
Pressed on, and stapled him against the upturned hull.
His dead jaw gaped. His soul
Crawled off his tongue and vanished into sunlight.

   Often at daybreak a salty moon
   Hangs over Ida; and the wind that comes
   Over the curve of the world from Asia
   Knocks a tile off Priam's roof.
   About this time each day for nine long years
   His men marched down the Skean road,
   Their spears like nettles stirred by wind.
   And round about this time each day
   The Greek commanders shade their eyes
   And squinny through the morning sun;
   And since no battle has returned
   All of its soldiers, the Trojans wave,
   Look back towards the Wall, and think
   Of those who may require new men next day.

The battle swayed.
Half-naked men hacked slowly at each other
As the Greeks eased back the Trojans.
   They stood close;
Closer; thigh in thigh; mask twisted over iron mask
Like kissing.
   One moment 50 chariots break out; head for the ditch;
Three cross; the rest wheel back; vanish in ochre dust.
For an instant the Greeks falter. One is killed. And then
The Trojans are eased back a little more;
The ship is cleared, the fire smothered, and who cares
That Hector's chariot opens a new way,
Now moving, pausing now, now moving on again,
And his spear's tip flickers in the smoky light
Like the head of a crested adder over fern?
Always the Trojans shift towards the ditch.

   Of several incidents, consider two:
Panotis' chariot yawed and tipped him
Back off the plate by Little Ajax' feet.
Neither had room to strike; and so the Greek
Knocked his head back with a forearm smash
And in the space his swaying made, close lopped.
Blood dulled both sides of the leafy blade.
Fate caught Panotis' body; death his head.
   Nearer the ditch Arcadeum met Lycon:
Catching each other's eye both cast, both missed,
Both ran together, and both struck; but
Only Lycon missed both times.
   His neck was cut clean through
Except for a skein of flesh off which
His head hung down like a melon.

   You will have heard about the restless mice

Called lemmings; how, at no set time, and why,
No one is sure, they form a grey cascade that pours
Out of the mountains, down, across the flat,
Until they rush into the sea and drown.

Likewise the Trojans as they crossed the ditch.

From the far bank Hector tried to help them.
Impossible . . .
   He did not guess
So many cars, so many infantry, had crossed;
Engaged, there never seemed enough; but now
They crammed the edge,
The big-eyed horses rearing at the drop,
Their mouths wrenched sideways,
Neck yokes dragged back like saddles.
   And though the drivers looped their reins,
Pegged themselves in, and hauled,
The teetering jam eased forward.
   Only the soft edge held them;
And as the wheels notched into it, the dirt came up
Over the bolts that pinned the axles to the centre-poles,
Horses on one side of the rim,
Cars and men the other.
   Stuck.
While other men, infantry,
Meant to be rearguard, climbed into, pulled friends into,
Shouted, struck at who tried to check them, jammed
Spear-poles through spokes—
   Aie . . .
And Patroclus let them, let them,
Let them balance, let them, then cried:
   "For Achilles!"
And drove in.

So the Trojans nearest to Patroclus squirmed
Away from him towards the ditch; and those
Near falling into it clawed back
Towards Patroclus; and those cram-packed between
Just clawed and squirmed until
The soft edge gave, and Ilium's combat chariotry
Toppled into the ditch like swill.

On certain winter days the land seems grey,
And the no-headroom left between it and the grey
Masses of downthrust cloud fills with wet haze:
Lines of cold rain weld mile on sightless mile
Of waste to air: floods occupy the state: and still
The rains continue, grey on grey:
God's punishment, say some, on those who bear
False witness, and some say, on those
Judges divorced from justice by contempt
Of those they judge: plus the accomplices of both
Perched on their fencing through the vacant day,
Until the water takes them all in all
In one enormous wave into the sea.

The Trojan horses made like this.
As they went up the far side of the ditch
They dragged behind them dead or half-dead charioteers
Looped in their reins.
Better like this, perhaps, than left to Greeks.

Patroclus split the rump.
Some (only a few) followed their horses up
Onto the plain and ran for Troy. The rest
Scurried along the ditch and hid themselves
Among Scamander's fens.

Nothing was left of Hector's victory except
Loose smoke-swaths like blue hair above the dunes,
And Panachea's ditch stained crimson where
Some outraged god five miles tall had stamped on glass.

A movement in the air. Gulls lift;
Then sideslip; land again. No more.
Mindless of everything Achilles said
Patroclus went for Troy.

See if you can imagine how it looked: A challenge

An opened fan, held flat; its pin
(That marks the ditch) towards yourself; its curve
(That spans the plain) remote:
The left guard points at Troy; the right
Covers the dunes that front the Aegean coast:
Like crabs disturbed by flame the Trojans run
This way and that across its radiants.
Patroclus thrusts his fighters at the mid
Point of the pleated leaf; a painted sun.

And it was here that Thestor, Enop's boy,
Met that circumstance in nature
Gods call Fate, and on this day, men called Patroclus.
   Thestor was not a Trojan.
But when King Priam's satraps came from Troy
And asked Sarpedon, Lycia's Prince, for aid,
And he said, "Yes"—Thestor, the apple of old Enop's eye,
Applied to leave his management and fight.
And as he reined away, he called:
   "Do not forsake me, O my seven meadows,

Until I conquer Greece!"
Though all he conquered was six foot of sand.

Fate's sister, Fortune, favours those
Who keep their nerve.
Thestor was not like this.
He lost his head, first; then his life.
His chariot bucked too slow over the rutted corpses
And as Patroclus drew abreast of him
The terrified boy let the horses baulk
Leaving the reins to flow beside his wheels
And cowered inside its varnished bodywork,
Weeping.
They passed so close that hub skinned hub.
Ahead, Patroclus braked a shade, and then,
And gracefully as men in oilskins cast
Fake insects over trout, he speared the boy,
And with his hip his pivot, prised Thestor up and out
As easily as later men detach
A sardine from an opened tin.

Nine more Lycians died on the long run for Troy,
And they were no great trouble.
If a spear missed, Patroclus watched
Their white heels flutter up the plain through dust,
Picked a fresh haft, waited, then pinned his next.
The day seemed done; dust could be left to dust;
Flies had laid eggs in many of the dead;
Until Sarpedon wedged his car across the rout,
Pushed up his mask, and said:
"Well run, my Lycians, but from what?"—
Selecting two light javelins—"Who will wait
To see their known Prince spit
Once and for all this big, anonymous Greek"—
And vaulted off his chariot plate—

"That makes you sweat?" then flexed himself,
Running his thumb across his points, and scuffed
Dirt toward Patroclus, who climbed down
More slowly; pleased beneath his iron.

It was noon.

God and His wife (who is His sister, too)
Watched them prepare. He, with regret; she,
With satisfaction heard Him out:
    "Surely Fate has marked enough good men without Sarpedon?
Shall I return him to his waving plains
Or let . . ."
    And she:
    "Others beside Yourself have children due today.
If one god saves his bud—why not the rest?
    My dear, I know You love Sarpedon; and I know
His death goes hard. Why not do this:
Let him fight bravely for a while; then, when
Patroclus severs him from care and misery,
Sleep and Death shall carry him to Lycia by Taurus,
Remembered by wise men throughout the world,
And buried royally."

Noon. Striped mosquitoes. Nothing stirs.

Under the white sun, back and forth
Across a disk of yellow earth, midway
Between the sea and the closed stone capital,
The heroes fought like Pharaoh's bare-necked hens
Wrangling over carrion in the air.
They sight each other, stand on their tails,
Lock claws, lie back inside their wings, and hang
High in between the white-faced pyramids
Each savaging the other's craw.

159

Likewise the human champions until
Patroclus' spear nosed past Sarpedon's busy heart
And the ground sense in his body leached away.
    Kneeling at first, then laid full length,
Teeth clenched and saying: "Gray, be quick
Or they will strip me while I live.
    And if they do it, if, Gray, if
My captured weapons prove their jubilee,
Shame on you, duke, until your dying day.
    So get our best.
Anaxapart, Aeneas, Hector, too—do not miss him—
And cover me with moving blades till sunset.
Then . . ." he was going,
"For my sake, fighter . . ." going,
"Kill!"
    And he was gone.
Sunlight reflecting in his dry brown eyes.
    Patroclus in his chariot again,
Wiping his neck, his smiling beard,
About to signal the advance.

    "Listen, Master!"
Gray prayed to Lord Apollo,
    "Wherever you may be,
    And you are everywhere,
    And everywhere you hear
    Men in their trouble;
    Trouble has come to me.
    Our best is dead and I
    Am wounded, Lord!
    O Lord Apollo hear my prayer!
    You know me, and you know
    That I shall fight until I die,
    But I can barely lift my arm!
    Lord, put my pain to sleep

160

And grant me strength enough to sweep
My pike across Sarpedon's corpse
Until the sun obeys your call to set."

And Apollo, Mousegod, Lord of the Morning, he
Whose face is brighter than a thousand suns,
Mollified his wound with sacred thought,
And let delight in fighting warm his loins.
And he did more: as Gray corralled their best,
Apollo called:
　"Sun, stand thou still over Ilium,
And guard Sarpedon's body till their blades
Move over it as grasses over stone."

　Air into azure steel;
The daylight stiffens to translucent horn;
　And through it
Falling
　One sun's cord
That opened out into a radiant cone around Sarpedon's corpse;
And him inside that light, as if
A god asleep upon his outstretched hand.

Dust like red mist.
Pain like chalk on slate. Heat like Arctic.
The light withdrawn from Sarpedon's body.
The enemies swirling over it.
Bronze flak.
　Man against man; banner behind raised banner;
The torn gold overwhelming the faded blue;
Blue overcoming gold; both up again; both frayed
By arrows that drift like bees, thicker than autumn rain.
　The left horse falls. The right, prances through blades,

Tearing its belly like a silk balloon.
And the shields inch forward under bowshots.
And under the shields the half-lost fighters think:
"We fight when the sun rises; when it sets we count the dead.
What has the beauty of Helen to do with us?" Half-lost,
With the ochre mist swirling around their knees,
They shuffle forward, lost, until the shields clash:
— A O I !
　　Lines of black ovals eight feet high, clash:
— A O I !
And in the half-light who will be first to hesitate,
Or, wavering, draw back, and Yes! . . . the slow
Wavering begins, and, Yes! . . . they bend away from us,
As spear points flicker between black hides
Bronze glows vaguely, and bones show like pink drumsticks.
　　And over it all,
As flies shift up and down a haemorrhage alive with ants,
The captains in their iron masks drift past each other,
Calling, calling, gathering light on their breastplates;
So stained they think that they are friends
And do not turn, do not salute, or else salute their enemies.
　　But we who are under the shields know
Our enemy marches at the head of the column;
And yet we march!
The voice we obey is the voice of the enemy;
Yet we obey!
And he who is forever talking about enemies
Is himself the enemy!

　　If Hector waved,
His wounded and his sick got up to fight;
And if Patroclus called, the Myrmidons
Struck, and called back; with them, as with Patroclus,
To die in battle was like going home.

Try to recall the pause, thock, pause,
Made by axe blades as they pace
Each other through a valuable wood.
Though the work takes place on the far
Side of a valley, and the axe strokes are
Muted by depths of warm, still standing, air,
They throb, throb, closely in your ear;
And now and then you catch a phrase
Exchanged between the men who work
More than a mile away, with perfect clarity.

Likewise the sound of spear on spear,
Shield against shield, shield against spear
Around Sarpedon's body.

And all this time God watched His favourite enemies:
Minute Patroclus, like a fleck
Of radium on His right hand,
Should he die now—or push the Trojans back still more?
And on His left, Prince Hector, like a silver mote.
    The right goes down.

    It is true that men are clever,
But the least of gods is cleverer than their best.
    And it was here, before God's hands
(Moons poised on either side of their earth's agate)
You overreached yourself, Patroclus.
    Yes, my darling,
Not only God was out that day but Lord Apollo.
"You know Apollo loves the Trojans: so,
Once you have forced them back, you stop."
    Remember it, Patroclus? Or was it years ago
Achilles cautioned you outside his tent?
    Remembering or not you stripped Sarpedon's gear
And went for Troy alone.

And God turned to Apollo, saying:
"Mousegod, take My Sarpedon out of range
And clarify his wounds with mountain water.
Moisten his body with tinctures of white myrrh
And violet iodine; and when these chrisms dry
Fold him in miniver that never wears
And lints that never fade
And call My two blind footmen, Sleep and Death,
To carry him to Lycia by Taurus,
Where, playing stone chimes and tambourines,
His group will consecrate his death,
Before whose memory the stones shall fade."
    And Apollo took Sarpedon out of range
And clarified his wounds with mountain water;
Moistened his body with tinctures of white myrrh
And violet iodine; and when these chrisms dried
He folded him in miniver and lints
That never wear, that never fade,
And called God's two blind footmen, Sleep and Death,
Who carried him
Before whose memory the stones shall fade
To Lycia by Taurus.

Three times Patroclus reached Troy's Wall.
Three times he leapt towards its parapet.
Three times, and every time he tried it on
The smiling Mousegod flicked him back.
But when he came a fourth, last time,
The smile was gone.
    Instead, from parapet to plain to beach-head, on,
Across the rucked, sunstruck Aegean, the Mousegod's voice,
Loud as ten thousand crying together,
Cried:

"Greek,
Get back where you belong!"

So loud
Even the Yellow Judges giving law
Half-way across the world's circumference paused.

"Get back where you belong!
Troy will fall in God's good time,
But not to you!"

It was Patroclus' turn to run, wide-armed,
Back from the Wall towards the dunes,
Staring into the fight, desperate to hide
(To blind that voice) to hide
Among the stainless blades.
    And as he ran for Leto's Chair,
Apollo dressed as Priam's brother, Kratex, stood
Above the Skean Gate, and strolled
Beside Andromache awhile, and took her arm,
Dissolving her anxiety with lies.
    Observe the scene:
They stand like relatives; the she, the god,
Chatting together on the terraces
Above the Gate.
    The elder points. The other nods. And his plumes nod
Over them both. In her mind's eye
Andromache can see her husband's spear
Entering Patroclus' stomach, while she hears
Apollo whispering:
"Achilles' heart will break . . ." And neither one
Thinks that a god discusses mortals with a mortal.

165

Patroclus fought like dreaming:
His head thrown back, his mouth—wide as a shrieking mask—
Sucked at the air to nourish his infuriated mind
And seemed to draw the Trojans onto him,
To lock them round his waist, red water, washed against his chest,
To lay their tired necks against his sword like birds.
—Is it a god? Divine? Needing no tenderness?—
Yet instantly they touch, he butts them,
Cuts them back:
—Kill them!
My sweet Patroclus,
—Kill them!
As many as you can,
   For
Coming behind you through the dust you felt
—What was it?—felt Creation part, and then

APO

LLO!

Who had been patient with you

Struck.

    His hand came from the east,
And in his wrist lay all eternity;
And every atom of his mythic weight
Was poised between his fist and bent left leg.
    Your eyes lurched out. Achilles' bonnet rang
Far and away beneath the cannon-bones of Trojan horses,
And you were footless . . . staggering . . . amazed . . .
Between the clumps of dying, dying yourself,
Dazed by the brilliance in your eyes,
The noise—like weirs heard far away—
Dabbling your astounded fingers
In the vomit on your chest.
    And all the Trojans lay and stared at you;
Propped themselves up and stared at you;
Feeling themselves as blest as you felt cursed.
    All of them lay and stared;
And one, a hero boy called Thackta, cast.
His javelin went through your calves,
Stitching your knees together, and you fell,
Not noticing the pain, and tried to crawl
Towards the Fleet, and—even now—feeling
For Thackta's ankle—ah!—and got it? No . . .
Not a boy's ankle that you got,
But Hector's.

    Standing above you,
His bronze mask smiling down into your face,
Putting his spear through . . . ach, and saying:
    "Why tears, Patroclus?
Did you hope to melt Troy down
And make our women fetch the ingots home?
    I can imagine it!
You and your marvellous Achilles;

170

Him with an upright finger, saying:
   'Don't show your face to me again, Patroclus,
Unless it's red with Hector's blood.'"
   And Patroclus,
Shaking the voice out of his body, says:
   "Big mouth.
Remember it took three of you to kill me.
A god, a boy, and, last and least, a hero.
   I can hear Death pronounce my name, and yet
Somehow it sounds like *Hector.*
   And as I close my eyes I see Achilles' face
With Death's voice coming out of it."

   Saying these things Patroclus died.
And as his soul went through the sand
Hector withdrew his spear and said:
   "Perhaps."

GBH

Faultless horizon. Flattish sea.
Wet shore. Wide plain. Look west:
   Cretan Merionez sees Patroclus fall,
And thinks: "His death will get us home."
   Under a mile away Prince Hector says:
"Thackta, keep watch,"
Who wants Achilles' chariot and pair.
Then climbs into his own. Full lock. And goes.

   Before it disappears beneath the sea
The plain due west of Troy accumulates
Into a range of whalebacked, hairy dunes,
Two days' ride long, parallel to the coast,
And, at their greatest, half a bowshot thick:
White, empty beaches, supervised by Greece,
Stretch from the tidemark to their crested cliffs;
But on the landward side, and long before
Their yellows fade through buff into the black
Alluvial plain supporting nearby Troy,
Sickle-shaped bays of deep, loose sand, embraced
By corniced horns, appear; and over there
—Much like the foothill of a parent range—
The knoll called Leto's Chair
Trespasses on the buff and masks the mouth
Of one such windless bay, in which
Patroclus lies and crouching Thackta dreams:

   "I got his love. If I could get his head . . ."

Picture a yacht
Canting at speed
Over ripple-ribbed sand.
  Change its mast to a man,
  Change its boom to a bow,
  Change its sail to a shield:
Notice Merionez
Breasting the whalebacks to picket the corpse of Patroclus.

Thackta, get lost: he has not seen you—yet;
A child beheading parsley grass
Is all you'll be to him, who knows—
If he can get it out—Patroclus' corpse
Will break Achilles' strike; an ample beast, who vaults
The tufted hussock between you and him
Then lets his long, grey, bronze-pronged spear
Sweep, sweep, Patroclus' vacant face; guarding him gone
Raptly as speechless breathers guard their young:
So run!
  But he does not. Prince Hector is his god.
Instead:
  "Cretan, get off my meat.
I got him first" (a lie) "his flesh is mine."
  Smooth as a dish that listens to the void
Merionez' face swings up.
  "Dear God," he thinks,
"Who is this lily-wristed titch?"
Picking a blob of dried froth from his lips,
Locking his mud-green eyes on Thackta's blue,
And saying: "Boy,
I can hear your heart.
Who hopes to hold your children on her knee?"

  Hector has found Achilles' sacred pair.
He idles in: "Hi'e . . . hi'e . . . ," his chariot in,

Dapple and grey they are, their reins in sand,
"Hi'e. Hi'e," who move away from him,
No hint of Troy or Thackta in his head.
　Air into lips; speech into Hector's ear;
Apollo's presence; Priam's voice: "My son,"
Who does not hear . . .
　Louder the god. The horses vanish. "Son,
Merionez has found Patroclus' corpse.
Thackta has just one spear."

　Whenever Thackta fought he wore
Slung from an oiled tendon round his neck
A cleverly articulated fish;
Each jacinth scale a moving part; each eye, a pearl.
His luck; his glittering christopher; a gift.
　"My name is Thackta, Crete," he said,
And fingered it.
　"Thackta, the son of Raphno, lord of Tus?"
"Indeed."
　"And brother of lord Midon?"
"Yes."
　"Here is the news. I killed him earlier today.
Not that his death was worth an ounce of fluff."
　Answer him, Thackta; keep him at his chat;
We can see Hector; Hector reads your fix
And will return before this king-sized wart
Upon the body of your world can cast,
So do not cast . . . And yet he does,
And notes—arm up, toe down—the spear approach
Merionez' needling mouth, who wills it near,
Observes it streaking through the sunburnt air,
Waits till its haft is half that haft's length off,
Then sheared it skyward with his own.
　And as that often polished leaf nosed out
Offhandedly the Cretan hero reached

For the tendon around Thackta's neck
Then smashed his downwards moving cry against his knee
And poached his eyes, and smashed and smashed
That baby face loose as a bag of nuts, and when
Young Thackta's whimpering gained that fine, high scream
Dear to a mind inspired by fearlessness, the Cretan duke
Posted his blade between the runny lips,
Increased the number of the dead by one,
Eased his malignant vigour with a sigh,
And scratched; then snapped the thong
And wiggled Thackta's jacinth fish
Between the sun and his heroic eye.

No sound. No movement in the bay.
Stripping his victim with professional speed.
Plate-straps between his teeth. Patroclus up.
And, hup! Knees bowed. One last look round.
Now up the whalebacks to the coast.

Not your day, king Merionez, not your day:
Dust in the air? or smoke? a shout—
Source out of sight, but near, but out of sight
Behind the crest, trough, crest, trough, crest,
Now soon, now soon to see
—Put down that armour, isolated lord—
Hector with Gray, Chylabborak, Anaxapart,
Outdistancing the wind that comes from Greece
—"If I leave you, Patroclus, what"—
And Hector's blood-cry, Hector's plume
—"If I do not, what will become of me?"—
Among the other, nodding plumes;
And all their banners rising one by one;
One after one; and then another one
—"Prince Hector's one of them"—

Come between Leto's Chair, the corniced horn,
Fast as a horned palm viper over tile,
Into the yellow bay.
   Bronze tyres. Reflecting breast-straps. You must set
Patroclus' body back upon the sand,
Then as the arrows start to splash, back off,
Running towards the backslope, up, a cat
Airborne a moment, one glance back: "Dear God,
Their chariots will slice," splash, "the corpse," splash, splash,
"In half," and reach the crest,
And:
   "Idomeneo!"
And:
   "Odysseus!"
You shout, and run, and run . . .
   And who would not?
   Then Hector's hand goes up.
Up go the horses. Zigzagged sand. Wheels lock.
   And you are off,
As he climbs down.
   Eyelight like sun on tin.
   "My lord?"
Turning Patroclus over with his foot,
   "Yes, champion Gray?" Looking up.
No sign of Troy therein.
   "The Greek has gone for help."
   "I know,"
His nostrils fluttering,
   "Give me your axe,"
His mouth like twine.
   "My axe?"
   "You, Manto:
Shell this lookalike and load the armour up."
   Tall plumes go bob.

"And you—"
(Sarpedon's armourer)
    "Anaxapart"
(Who once had 50 stitches in his face)
    "Up with its shoulders. Yes, like that."
(And you could strike a match upon the scar.)
    "Now stretch its neck across that rock,"
His arm held out behind; still looking down:
    "Lord Gray, I asked you for your axe."
Zephyrs disturb their gilded crests. Mask meets mask.
Then Gray:
    "Before you use Patroclus' fat to grease
Your chariot hubs, Overlord Hector, ask yourself how
Troy can be held without Sarpedon's men.

    Dog in the forehead but at heart a deer,
Recall the luckless morning when you kicked
Your silk-and-silver counterpane aside
And found your coast alive with shrieking Greeks.

    After the shock of it, was not Sarpedon's name
The first to cross your lips? whose help you begged?
Though all you sent was '*We would be obliged*'
And '*Thankyou, thankyou*' when he promised it—
Keeping his promise with half Lycia.

    And on the day we came,
Before Aeneas and yourself had stopped
Mow multiplying thanks by previous thanks
Sarpedon and Anaxapart had armed,
Gotten our troops together and engaged.

    That day, and every long successive fighting day,
He was first out, last home; with laughter,
Golden wounds, good words; always the first,
First across Agamemnon's ditch today.

    But now that he is dead and has no fellow,
How do you keep your obligation, Hector?

Begging my axe to violate the one
Greek corpse sufficiently revered to change for his,
Wanting Achilles' gear to pod your beef,
And giving Merionez the time to fetch
More of our enemies up.
　　I know . . . I know . . ."
Ingathering his reins:
　　"Day one, a friend; day two, a guest; day three, a chore.
Sarpedon's death makes me the Lycian chief.
Why should we risk ourselves for Hector's Wall
Who leaves his ally naked on the sand?"

　　Thin
Wavering heat. Big flakes of sand. Live things
Blown right and left.
　　The tail-end of a banner wraps
A soldier's face.

　　"You will not die saluting, will you, Gray?"
Prince Hector said. And to the rest:
　　"Get the bones home. When Greece comes back
I shall be good enough to watch."

　　Patroclus naked now.
The mirror bronze beneath a chariot rug.
Manto beside the horses, eyes cast down,
Awaiting Hector's word.

　　"Lead on."

　　Silent as men grown old while following sheep
They watch him wheel away.

Sea-bird's eye view:
Soldiers around Patroclus: centaur ants
Hoisting a morsel,
    And,
On the whalebacks' tidal side,
Idomeneo, Ajax, Little A.,
Odysseus and his driver, Bombax, head
A wedge of plate-faced Greeks.
    Close-up on Bombax; 45; fighting since 2;
Who wears his plate beneath his skin; one who has killed
More talking bipeds than Troy's Wall has bricks;
Whose hair is long, is oiled, is white, is sprung,
Plaited with silver wire, twice plaited—strong?—
Why, he could swing a city to and fro with it
And get no crick; whose eye can fix
A spider's web yoking a tent peg to its guy
Five miles downbeach—and count its spokes:
    "By night?"
    See them come padding down the coastal lane,
Flow up the low-browed, crested cliffs, across the backs;
Two hundred plus; then, at Odysseus' sign, drop flat,
And steer their chin-straps through the sabre grass,
Lining the shoulders of the bay to look
Down from the Chair at Gray beside Patroclus' corpse.
    "Ready?" Odysseus says.
Their eye-holes nod.

Moving at speed, but absolutely still,
The arrow in the air. Death in a man
As something first perceived by accident.
    Massed leaves; massed glare;
The piston-kneed, blade-flailing Greeks pour down
Like a gigantic fan with razored vanes,

Leaping the hummock-studded slope, up-down,
As if the ground between each clump was taut,
Was trampoline, up-down, so slow they fly,
So quick upon the sand.
      Gray for an instant blinded by the sky
White backflash off their sand-scoured front; but in the next,
Scanning them through its after-image, cool
As the atrium of a mossy shrine, and shouts:
      "Close! Close!"
Too late, alas. Before his voice is out
Their masks are on him like a waterfall!
      Who was it said
That one long day's more work will see it done?
Up to the waist in dead:
      "Dear Lord of Mice," he prays,
      "Dear Lord," his soldiers dead,
      "By day,"
Their souls like babies rising from their lips,
      "A river in the sky,"
"Keep close!"
      "By night, an Amazon.
      Save us from this and I will build a stone"
"Close! Closer still!"
      "Temple that bears"
"Now slope your shields!"
      "Shadows of deer at sunset and thy name."
      Clenching his men about Patroclus' corpse;
Faced by a fly; all eyes; an egg with eyes;
"We have it still!"—attacked by eyes—"Edge out . . ."
Arrows that thock, that enter eyes, that pass
Close as a layer of paint, that blind,
That splash about them like spring rain.
      Bombax takes heads
Like chopping twelve-inch logs for exercise;
Feathers of blood surround him like a nude

On decorative water; "Hector, where?—
Dog in the forehead but at heart a doe,"
As sunlight jumps from cheek to shiny cheek,
Eager to glorify their transience.
    "Not up the Chair, that way lies death,
Anaxapart," who does not hear, his eyes
On Pyrop, "the Athenian Ham" (as Little Ajax christened him)
The richest and the fattest Greek
(A chariot factory plus numerous farms)
To sail to Ilium from Aulis;
Who looks behind him, half crouched down,
As timid and as fearful as a dog
About to shit.
    "Run, Greek—run, run,"
Anaxapart insists. And (fool!) instead
Of burrowing among the shields, he does,
And running cries:
    "My mother is alone, and old, and sick,"
But what fear urged obesity held back.
Six arrows in the Lycian's fist:
    "My"—one
    "Is"—two
    "And"—three

    Then —four—five—six
In the air at once . . .   Wi'eeee!
Even Odysseus paused to catch that trick.
—And the arrows go so fast their shanks ignite!
—And the hits make Pyrop flounce!
—And he cannot hold his mud!
Six hammer blows upon his neck; and long before his voice,
So high, so piteous and profound, died out,
Anaxapart's keen zanies sheared his tin.
    Pleasure maybe
But not a sign of victory in this.

Gray shows red:
Bent as if seen through water, split tip hooked,
Both edges blunted on Greek flesh, his leaf.
  "This is our end, my Lord,"
His feet go backwards, treading on the dead
That sigh and ooze like moss.
  "Heaven is silent;
  Earth does not confide;
  I turn around,
  The way to Troy is barred."
Patroclus in their midst. Around him, shields.
Around the shields, the mouth-hole masks.
  "Close! Close!"

Achilles' armour was not made on earth.
The lame god yoked its spacious particles.
Deliberate inattention has
Only enhanced its light-collecting planes;
Into whose depth, safe, safe, amid the dunes
Prince Hector looks, amazed, and strips his own;
Stands naked in the light, amazed, and lifts
Its bodice up, and kisses it; then holds it out,
And, like a man long kept from water, lets
Its radiance pour down; and sees within
The clouds that pass, the gulls that stall,
His own hope-governed face, and near its rim,
Distorted as the brilliant surface bends
Its rivetless, near-minus weight away,
His patient horses, and his men.

  Then,
Through the azure vacancy in which
Our cooling onion floats: clouds long as lips,

God's lips above the mountain, saying:
   "Worm:
Your death is nearer than your nose.
'Perhaps,' you told Patroclus as he went.
Perhaps was wrong. But I will let you fight
Dressed as the gods are dressed,
And give your heart a priceless boost until
Oblivion's resistless whisper bids
Its pulse (a drum between two torches in the night)
To follow your creation on their way."

One thousand Trojan soldiers form a ring.
They link their arms; they breathe in unison;
Lay back their faces till each throat stands wide,
And wait. And wait. Then on the masterbeat,
Shatter the empyrean with a cry!
Then stamp! Then cry! Then stamp again! Then cry!
Cry overfollowing cry, concordant stamp
On stamp, until the far, translucent hue
Augments their promising to die, and rides
Forward to sunset on their "God for Troy!"
   Hector is in the middle of that ring;
Crouched on his toes; his knees braced wide; palms up;
White dactyls tigered; arms outspread.
And now his certain, triple-armoured mind
(By God, the holy metal, and his men)
Grows light, grows lucent, clarified for death.
And as their voices mix above their prince,
He rocks from toe to toe; and as they stamp,
First one and then the other of his feet
Lifts from the sand; and as they lean and lead
Into a skip-step sunwise traipse around,

Though Hector keeps his body jack-knifed down,
Adding his voice to theirs he starts to turn
Counter their turn, to lift himself, to spin,
Becoming in their eyes a source, a sun,
A star, whose force is theirs, who leaps—
Unfolds his body in the air,
Prances upon the air, and in the air
Unsheathes Achilles' sword and makes it sing . . .
    See how they flow towards him, arms upraised,
Table their shields to keep his dance aloft,
And cry again, and cry, and start to pour
Over the dunes, him spinning on that top,
Across the buff and onward to the bay,
Achilles' blade about his waist, so fast,
A cymbal struck by voices, shimmer struck,
Out of whose metal centre Hector's own,
Seething between his teeth, wails up the sky
On one insatiable note.
    And as his wail spread outward on the air,
And as the stolen armour ate the light,
Those fighting round Patroclus' body thought
Earth had upthrust a floe of luminous malt
That swamped their world and pitched the famous Greeks
Back to the crest and filled the bay with waves.
    And surfacing upon that molten sludge,
Gray in his arms, Prince Hector said,
As he wiped the crawling stains away:
    "Remember me?"
Aeneas going by so close
His slipstream pats their cheeks
    "Remember me?"
And rings Patroclus with a horse-high
Set-too-close-for-the-point-of-a-spear's-tip
Wall of a hundred oxhide shields.

Impacted battle. Dust above a herd.
Trachea, source of tears, sliced clean.
Deckle-edged wounds: "Poor Jataphact, to know," knocked clean
Out of his armour like a half-set jelly
"Your eyes to be still open yet not see," or see
By an abandoned chariot a dog
With something like your forearm in its mouth;
A face split off,
Sent skimming lidlike through the crunch
Still smiling, but its pupils dots on dice:
   Bodies so intermixed
The tremor of their impact keeps the dead
Upright within the mass. Half-dragged, half-borne,
Killed five times over, Captol—rose with his oar,
Sang as his rapt ship ran its sunside strake
Through the lace of an oncoming wave—now splashed
With blood plus slaver from his chest to chin,
Borne back into the mass, itself borne back
And forth across the bay like cherry froth.
   Someone breaks out; another follows him;
Throws, hits, rides on; the first—transfixed—
Hauls on the carefully selected pole
Trembling within his groin, and drags
His bladder out with it;
Then doubles popeyed back into the jam.
   Notice the cousins, Little A. & Big—some team!
Prince Little loves to tease them with his arse:
   "I'll screw your widow, Pellity,"
Shouting head down, his face between his knees;
And when the angered Trojan throws, *he* throws,
Twisting and catching what the other threw
And has the time to watch his leaf divide
His fellow soldier from the light, then goes
"No third green generation from *his* tree,"

Whistling away.
   The Greeks swear by their dead. The Trojans by their home.
"Not one step back—" "If I should die—" and does.
Water through water: who can tell whose red, whose roar
It is? Their banners overclouding one by one;
One after one; and then another one.
   Anaxapart has tied Patroclus' body to a shield:
Spreadeagled on its front
With Zeeteez and Opknocktophon as crucifers.
And much as their posterity will spurn
Vampires with garlic, ignorance with thought,
Those Trojans elevate his corpse and claim:
   "Gangway for Troy!"
While in the chariot length their idol gains,
With fingerbells and feathered necklacing,
Molo the Dancer from Cymatriax
Tugs at its penis as he squeaks:
   "Achilles' love!"
   Trumpets behind the corpse. More Trojan masks.
Then tambourines and drums: "Not one step back . . ."
But must! "Troy!" "Troy!" "If I—" and does,
And all: "Are these my arms,
So tired they go on, and on, alone?"

   Seeking a quiet eddy in the flood.
Blood flowing from his nostrils. He who fights
Without the aid of anger says: "Antilochos.
Run to the Fleet. Give Wondersulk our news.
His love is dead. His armour gone.
Prince Hector has the corpse. And as an afterthought
That we are lost."
   "Why me, Odysseus?"
   "That is the why. Now go—
And not so gloomy if you wish to please."
   Fast as the strongest wing can fly

Between the twilight and the setting sun,
He goes.

Elsewhere late afternoon goes lazily enough.
No sign of cloud. Small noises cross the air intact.
    And yawning as he leaves his tent
To sigh and settle back against a rope
(As some men settle into life
Quiet in quiet rooms, supplied
With all they need by mute, obedient hands)
Achilles: doing his best to blimp
The queasy premonitions that explode beneath his heart:
    "No matter how, how much, how often, or how easily you win—
O my Patroclus, are you bitten off?"

    Antilochos appearing through these words.
Hateful the voice that springs between his clear-edged lips
Weakening Odysseus' message to: "Is gone."

    Down on your knees, Achilles. Farther down.
Now forward on your hands and put your face into the dirt
And scrub it to and fro.
    Grief has you by the hair with one
And with the forceps of its other hand
Uses your mouth to trowel the dogshit up;
Watches you lift your arms to Heaven; and then
Pounces and screws your nose into the filth.
    Gods have plucked drawstrings from your head
And from the template of your upper lip
Modelled their bows.
    Not now. Not since
Your grieving reaches out and pistol-whips
That envied face, until

Frightened to bear your black, backbreaking agony alone,
You sank, throat back, thrown back, your voice
Thrown out across the sea to reach your Source.

Salt-water woman
Eternal
   She heard him
Long-bodied Thetis who lives in the wave
   In the coral
   Fluorescent
Green over grey over olive forever
   The light falling sideways from Heaven
She heard him
   Achilles
Her marvellous son.

   Surge in her body.
Head ferns grow wider
   Grow paler.
Her message   his message
   Goes through the water:
   "Sisters,"
Nay'rúesay,
   "Sisters,"
Eternal
   Salt-water women
Came when she called to them
Came through the waves to her   swam as she swam
Towards Greece, beyond Greece, now she passes the Islands
Arm over arm swimming backways, peaked nipples,
Full 50 green-grey palely shimmering kith of King Nay'rúce,
Those who leave eddies, who startle, her sisters:
   Derna, Leucaté, lithe Famagusta,

Isso, Nifaria, black chevroned Cos,
Panopay, beaded, entwining Galethiel,
Thasos, Talitha, Hymno and Phylé,
Sleek Manapharium, Jithis, Bardia,
Serpentine Xanthe, Nemix and Simi,
Came from the iodine   surfaced through azure
Onto the beach-head and lay round Achilles.

"What cause have you to weep?" his mother said.
"It was your hands God saw, your voice He heard
Uplifted, saying: *'Lord, until they feel my lack,
Let the Greeks burn; let them taste pain.'*"
    And heard him say:

    "Poor Source,
That dowry of Heaven-sent weapons you brought
My father when Our Father saw
You had protected His omnipotence
Pods Hector now; and I, the paradigm
Of all creation's violent hierarchy,
Sit naked by the sea and number waves.
    Excellent that my Greekish aides taste pain;
And better that they die. But not enough.
Not agony enough. Increase that pain.
Without appeal and without delay
Let death come down—and not, please God
(For I will be His servant either way)
Exclusively to Agamemnon's led:
But onto Troy; and onto Troy Beyond; and unto all of us
Brain-damaged, stinking herd of God-foxed sheep,
Chiefs of our loathsome, thought-polluted dot,
Bar two: Hector's dark head is mine."
    "You cannot have it without armour, child,"
His mother said,
And vanished through the waves with all her school.

192

Sunfade. Sea breathing. Sea-lice trot
Over warm stones.
     Achilles and Antilochos:
How small they look beneath the disappearing sky!
     Sap rises in them both. An opening breeze
Ruffles their hair; but only A. hears:

     "Greek . . ."
     "Yes?"
     "Greek . . ."
     "Who?"
     "Iris."
     "Speak."
     "Go to the ditch.
Let Troy know you are back.
Until your strength is operational
Your voice must serve.
     You know what fighting is:
When things are at their worst
An extra shout can save the day."

     He goes.

Consider planes at touchdown—how they poise;
Or palms beneath a numbered hurricane;
Or birds wheeled sideways over windswept heights;
Or burly salmon challenging a weir;
Right-angled, dreamy fliers, as they ride
The instep of a dying wave, or trace
Diagonals on snowslopes:

Quick cuts like these may give
Some definition to the mind's wild eye

That follow-spots Achilles' sacred pair—
No death, no dung, no loyalty to man
In them—come Troyside down the dunes towards the Chair, the bay,
Achilles' charioteer, Alastor, lost
On their basket's plate, locked to their reins,
Pulling with all his might to make them stay,
That also Iris heard, that know their Care,
Their semi-human Clay, their half-loved, half-obeyed,
Half-childlike lord, Achilles, will soon call.

Head-lock, body-slam,
Hector attacking;
    His anger, his armour, his:
"Now, now, or never, O Infinite, Endless Apollo,"
    But silent,
    "In my omnipotence I beg to cast
All thought of peace on earth for me away
Until I own that corpse."
    Hard to say who is who: the fighters, the heroes,
Their guts look alike.

    Ajax alone between it and their thirst:
Pivoting on his toes, his arms looped up,
Safe in his hands his spear's moist butt, that whirrs
—Who falls into that airscrew, kiss goodbye—
And for a moment Hector driven back,
And when, and if, and here it comes:
"On! On! On! On!" he cries. "Die on that spear!"
The Trojans try to snake beneath its point,
And Ajax down on one, and with the other foot
Thrusts himself round until the spear's bronze torque
Hisses a finger's width above Patroclus' face,

As Bombax shouts: "Here, Ajax, here,"
As Menelaos: "Here . . ."

Aeneas through the blades, brushing their strokes aside,
Up the far slope, with Ajax far behind,
And sees Alastor entering the bay
Between the horn and Leto's Chair,
And sprints towards its brink,
And . . .   off!—
   Free fall—
   Free fall—
Swooping towards Alastor in his car,
As angels in commemorative stone
Still swoop on unknown soldiers as they die
For some at best but half-remembered cause.
   And as Alastor swerved, Aeneas' axe
Enhanced the natural crackage of his skull,
And he quit being, while his pair
Skid-slithered through the tumult, flailed that mass,
And overran Patroclus' tattered corpse.

   Hector triumphant:
Dropping his spear, clenching his fists,
Raising his fists in the air, shaking his fists with delight:
   "Who brings it out will share the fame with me!"

   Anaxapart has got it by the chin.
Knees bent, spine bowed, feet braced into the clavicles,
Wrenching the nut right left right right, thinks:
"Screw the bastard off . . ."
Leaning across Anaxapart Prince Hector shouts, "On! On!"
Trying to slash at Bombax and the Greeks,
Who have Patroclus by the feet, and tug:
   "Ah . . ."

They tug.
  "Ah . . ."
The body stretched between them like a hide.

Look north.
Achilles on the rampart by the ditch:
  He lifts his face to 90; draws his breath;
And from the bottom of his heart emits
So long and loud and terrible a scream,
The icy scabs at either end of earth
Winced in their sleep; and in the heads that fought
It seemed as if, and through his voice alone,
The whole world's woe could be abandoned to the sky.

And in that instant all the fighting glassed.

Thoal excepted.

  Quick as a priest who waits for passing birds
To form a letter in the air
He has Patroclus' body up and out.
  And as Prince Hector shouts:
"The Greeks have got their carrion intact!"
  The sun,
Head of a still-surviving kingdom, drew
The earth between them and himself,
  And so the plain grew dark.

Starred sky. Calm sky.
Only the water's luminosity
Marks the land's end.

A light is moving down the beach.
It wavers. Comes towards the fleet.
The hulls like upturned glasses made of jet.

Is it a god?

No details

Yet.

Now we can hear a drum.

And now we see it:
Six warriors with flaming wands,
Eight veteran bearers, and one prince,
Patroclus, dead, crossed axes on his chest,
Upon a bier.

Gold on the wrists that bear the prince aloft.
Tears on the cheeks of those who lead with wands.
Multiple injuries adorn the corpse.
And we, the army, genuflect in line.

Having destroyed the town of Thebé-under-Ida
Achilles kept its temple's cauldron for himself.
Talthibios deciphered the inscriptions on its waist.
One said:
I AM THE EARTH
The other:
VOID.

And when from zigzagged ewers his female slaves
Had filled and built a fire beneath its knees,

Achilles laved the flesh and pinned the wounds
And dressed the yellow hair and spread
Ointments from Thetis' cave on every mark
Of what Patroclus was, and kissed its mouth,
And wet its face with tears, and kissed and kissed again,
And said: "My love, I swear you will not burn
Till Hector's severed head is in my lap."

Pax

Rat.
Pearl.
Onion.
Honey.
These colours came before the sun
Lifted above the ocean,
Bringing light
Alike to mortals and Immortals.

  And through this falling brightness
Through the by now
Mosque
Eucalyptus
Utter blue
Came Thetis,
Gliding across the azimuth,
With armour the colour of moonlight laid on her forearms,
Palms upturned,
Hovering above the Fleet,
Her skyish face towards her son

  Achilles
Gripping the body of Patroclus
Naked and dead against his own,
While Thetis spoke:
  "Son . . ."
His soldiers looking on;
Looking away from it; remembering their own:
  "Grieving will not amend what Heaven has done.
Suppose you throw your hate after Patroclus' soul.

Who besides Troy will gain?
    See what I've brought . . ."

    And as she laid the moonlit armour on the sand
It chimed;
    And the sound that came from it
Followed the light that came from it
Like sighing
Saying:
    Made in Heaven.

    And those who had the neck to watch Achilles weep
Could not look now.
    Nobody looked. They were afraid.

    Except Achilles: looked,
Lifted a piece of it between his hands;
Turned it; tested the weight of it; and then
Spun the holy tungsten like a star between his knees,
Slitting his eyes against the flare, some said,
But others thought the hatred shuttered by his lids
Made him protect the metal.

    His eyes like furnace doors ajar.

    When he had got its weight
And let its industry console his grief a bit:
    "I'll fight,"
He said. Simple as that. "I'll fight."

    And so Troy fell.

    "But while I fight, what will become of this"—
Patroclus—"mother?

Inside an hour a thousand slimy things will burrow.
And if the fight drags on his flesh will swarm
Like water boiling."
        And she:
"Son, while you fight,
Nothing shall taint him;
Sun will not touch him,
Nor the slimy things."

        Promising this she slid
Rare ichors in the seven born openings of Patroclus' head
Making the carrion radiant.
        And her Achilles went to make amends,
Walking alone beside the broken lace that hung
Over the sea's green fist.

        The sea that is always counting.

Ever since men began in time, time and
Time again they met in parliaments,
Where, in due turn, letting the next man speak,
With mouthfuls of soft air they tried to stop
Themselves from ravening their talking throats;
Hoping enunciated airs would fall
With verisimilitude in different minds,
And bring some concord to those minds; soft air
Between the hatred dying animals
Monotonously bear towards themselves;
Only soft air to underwrite the in-
Built violence of being, to meld it to
Something more civil, rarer than true forgiveness.
No work was lovelier in history;

And nothing failed so often: knowing this
The army came to hear Achilles say:
"Pax, Agamemnon." And Agamemnon's: "Pax."

Now I must ask you to forget reality,
To be a momentary bird above those men
And watch their filings gather round
The rumour of a conference until
Magnetic grapevines bind them close.
    From a low angle the army looks oval, whitish centered,
Split at one end, prised slightly open, and,
Opposite to the opening, Achilles
(Who they have come to hear) with hard-faced veterans
On either side, lance-butts struck down,
And here and there a flag. Even the chariot body-shop,
Physiotherapists and unclaimed shes
Came to the common sand to hear their lords say pax.

And as men will, they came, the limping kings;
Odysseus first, chatting to Menelaos, through the ring,
Sitting them down; and after them, a trifle slow
But coming all the same, doomed Agamemnon,
King of kings, his elbow gummed with blood.

    The ring is shut. Enormous calm.
King Agamemnon and Achilles face to face,
Distinct as polygon and square.

    Achilles first:
"King,
I have been a fool.
The arid bliss self-righteousness provokes
Addled my mind."
    Odysseus nods.
"Remembering how I took Briseis' town,

It would have been far better for us both
If Artemis had pinned her to its gates.
And doubtless as their mouths filled up with dust
The Greeks who died in our black amnesty
Wished she had done.
    Yet I'm a man. I like my own.
And if another man—my King, what's more—
Takes what is mine and lets the army know it,
What are they both to do?
    Kings can admit so little.
Kings know: what damages their principality
Endangers all.
    If he is inconsiderate,
He is the King; if greedy, greedy King,
And if at noon the King says: 'It is night.'—
Behold, the stars!
    What if he damages the man
On whom his principality depends?
He's still the King. His war goes on. The man must give.
    But if the man in question cannot give
Because the god in him that makes the King his chief dependant
Is part and parcel of the god that cries *Revenge!* when he is wronged,
What happens then?
    Stamp on my foot, my heart is stunned;
I cannot help it; it is stunned; it rankles—
Here," touching his chest.
    "I am not angry anymore.
My heart is broken. Done is done, it says.
And yet its pain can only mask my rancour.
So let pride serve.
When all is said and done—I am Achilles."

    And the army love their darling, and they cry:
"Achil! Achil! Achil!"

Louder than any counting sea;
And sentries on the Wall sweat by their spears.

King Agamemnon waits.

And waits.

Then rising, says:

"Heroes . . .
I do not think your zeal will be injured
If those who are the farthest off stand still,
And those in front stop muttering to themselves."
    Bad start.
"Everyone can't hear everything, of course."
    Gulls cry.
"However, even clear-voiced heralds,
Accustomed as they are to public speaking,
Can lose their audience if inattention makes them feel
Indifference to their message."
    Gulls.

    "In fact, the things I have to say are, in a sense,
Meant for Achilles' ears alone.
But if the army and his peers witness our settlement
My purpose will be better served.
    Like him, I am a man.
But I am also King. His King. Your King.
And as your King I have received
What most of you have not unwillingly agreed was mine:
The best part of the blame."
    He has them now.
    "BUT I AM NOT TO BLAME!"
    And now.
"Undoubtedly I took, unfairly, pulling rank,

The girl Achilles won.
I tell you it was not my wish.
Between my judgement and my action Ahtay fell;
God's eldest girl, contentious Ahtay . . . Oh,
Soft are her footsteps but her performance keeps no day;
Nor does she walk upon the ground, but drifts
Into our human wishes like the sticky flecks of down
Tickling our lips in endless summertime;
And with her episode comes misery.
   Let me remind you how God walked
Into the courtyard of the sun and told His co-eternals:
   'Drink with me!
   For unto men this day a child is born
   Whose blood is royal with My eminence;
   And who, all in good time, will be
   A king called *Hercules*.'
And looking at her fingers, Hera said:
   'We have been fooled before.
   However; if You swear
   That any child of Yours born on this day . . .'
God swore; and Ahtay sat between His eyes.
Soon as the oath had crossed His mythic lips
Hera went quick as that from Heaven to Greece,
And with her right hand masked the womb
Swaddling Hercules, and with her left
Parted the body of another girl whose child was His
But only eight months gone,
And held it up and jeered:
   'See what your oath has done!'
   God made the early boy a king, and Hercules a serf
And wept as men must weep.
   If you will lead the Greeks, Achilles,
I will give Briseis back;
   And may we be forgiven."

The sun is smaller now.

Achilles says: "Let us fight now—*at once*—"

"Wait"—slipping the word in like a bolt—
"Marvellous boy," Odysseus says.
    "You can do what you like with us except make men fight hungry.
    Well . . . you could do that too, but . . ."
Turning away from him towards the ranks:
    "Wait!
The King will keep his promise now.
Young lords will fetch his penal gifts
For everyone to see and be amazed.
    Everyone knows that men who get
Angry without good reason will
Conciliate without free gifts.
    Therefore Achilles gladly takes
Everything Agamemnon gives.
    And he who gives steps free of blame,
As he adopts the wrong.
    God bless them both."

    Then squatting by Achilles, says:
"Boy—you are the best of us. Your strength is fabulous.
Let me play wise.
    What we have got to do is not embroidery.
For you, the battle may be gold.
The men will enter it like needles
Breaking or broken, but either way
Emerging naked as they went.
    Think of the moment when they see
The usual loot is missing from this fight
Although the usual risks are not.
They do not own the swords with which they fight,
Nor the ships that brought them here;

Orders are handed down to them in words
They barely understand.
They do not give a whit who owns queen Helen.
Ithaca's mine; Pythia yours; but what are they defending?
They love you? Yes. They do. They also loved Patroclus.
And he is dead, they say. Bury the dead, they say.
A hundred of us singing angels died for every knock
Patroclus took—so why the fuss?—that's war, they say,
Who came to eat in Troy and not to prove how much
Dear friends are missed.
    Certainly, they are fools.
But they are right. Fools often are.
    Bury the dead, Achil,
And I will help you pitch Troy in the sea."

Cobalt in Heaven
And below it
    Polar blue.
The body of the air is lapis, and
    Where it falls
Behind the soft horizon
The light turns back to Heaven.

    A soldier pisses by his chariot.
Another
    Sweetens his axe blade on a soapy stone.
And up between the dunes,
With ribbons, tambourines, and little drums,
Come twelve white horses led by seven women
Briseis in their midst
Her breasts so lovely that they envy one another:
    And they pass by:
And after them young lords escorting

Twenty ewers of bright silver each in a polished trivet
Their shining cheeks engraved by silversmiths
With files of long-nosed soldiers on the march:
   And they pass by:
And after them a sledge
Piled with twelve lots of Asian gold
Carefully weighed, worth a small city:
   And they pass by:
And last of all, guarding a sacrificial hog,
Talthibios passed by into the centre of the ring.

   Yellow mists over Mount Ida.
The hog lowers its gilded tusks.
Is still.

   By Agamemnon's feet Talthibios sprinkles barley,
Snips a tuft from the hog's nape,
Waits for a breeze to nudge it off his palm
Into the flames that burn between the army and its King.

   Haze covers Ida.
Sand falls down sand.
Even the gods are listless.

   And Agamemnon spreads his arms,
Raises his face towards the sun, and cries:

   "GOD
   Be my witness.
   EARTH
   My witness.
   SUN, SKY, WATER, WIND
   My witness.
   I have not tampered with the girl
   I took unjustly from Achilles."

Then drags his knife across the hog's silk throat.

Mists over Ida.

Slaves gut and throw the dead hog in the sea.

The army like ten thousand yellow stones.

    Achilles says:
"So be it.
Eat, and prepare to fight."

And took Briseis to his ship.

Under the curve the keel makes
Where it sweeps upright to the painted beak
Achilles' heroes placed their gilded oars
Set twelve carved thwarts across them
Surfaced this stage with wolf- and beaver-fleece
Amid whose stirring nap Patroclus lay
The damaged statue of a prince awaiting transportation.
    Near it Achilles sat, Odysseus beside,
And women brought them food.
    "Patroclus liked to eat," Achilles said,
"And you cooked well, Patroclus, didn't you?
Particularly well that summer when
My cousin Ajax and king Nestor drove
Up from the Pel'ponnesus crying 'wife'
And 'theft' and 'war' and 'please' and
What is this 'eat' of yours, Odysseus?
If you were telling me: He's dead, your father; well,
I might eat a bit; troubled, it's true; but eat
Like any fool who came God knows how many mist

And danger mixed sea miles to repossess fair Helen.
    I know you, Ithaca: you think:
Achilles will fight better if he feeds.
Don't be so sure.
    I do not care about his gifts. I do not care, Odysseus,
Do not care.
    Patroclus was my life's sole love.
The only living thing that called
Love out of me.
At night I used to dream of how, when he came home to Greece,
He'd tell them of my death—for I must die—and show my son
This house, for instance, or that stone beside the stream,
My long green meadows stretching through the light
So clear it seems to magnify . . ."

    And here Achilles falls asleep beside his dead;
And king Odysseus goes off as close to tears
As he will ever be.

    Now I shall ask you to imagine how
    Men under discipline of death prepare for war.
    There is much more to it than armament,
    And kicks from those who could not catch an hour's sleep
    Waking the ones who dozed like rows of spoons;
    Or those with everything to lose, the kings,
    Asleep like pistols in red velvet.
    Moments like these absolve the needs dividing men.
    Whatever caught and brought and kept them here
    Under Troy's Wall for ten burnt years
    Is lost: and for a while they join a terrible equality,
    Are virtuous, self-sacrificing, free:
    And so insidious is this liberty
    That those surviving it will bear
    An even greater servitude to its root:
    Believing they were whole, while they were brave;

That they were rich, because their loot was great;
That war was meaningful, because they lost their friends.
They rise!—the Greeks with smiling iron mouths.
They are like Nature; like a mass of flame;
Great lengths of water struck by changing winds;
A forest of innumerable trees;
Boundless sand; snowfall across broad steppes at dusk.
As a huge beast stands and turns around itself,
The well-fed, glittering army, stands and turns.

Nothing can happen till Achilles wakes.

He wakes.

Those who have slept with sorrow in their hearts
Know all too well how short but sweet
The instant of their coming-to can be:
The heart is strong, as if it never sorrowed;
The mind's dear clarity intact; and then,
The vast, unhappy stone from yesterday
Rolls down these vital units to the bottom of oneself.

Achilles saw his armour in that instant
And its ominous radiance flooded his heart.
   Bright pads with toggles crossed behind the knees,
Bodice of fitted tungsten, pliable straps;
His shield as round and rich as moons in spring;
His sword's haft parked between sheaves of grey obsidian
From which a lucid blade stood out, leaf-shaped, adorned
With running spirals.
   And for his head a welded cortex; yes,
Though it is noon, the helmet screams against the light;
Scratches the eye; so violent it can be seen
Across three thousand years.

Achilles stands; he stretches; turns on his heel;
Punches the sunlight, bends, then—jumps! . . .
And lets the world turn fractionally beneath his feet.

Noon. In the foothills
Melons emerge from their green hidings.
Heat.

He walks towards the chariot.
Greece waits.

Over the wells in Troy mosquitoes hover.

Beside the chariot.
Leading the sacred horses; watching his this-day's driver, Automedon,
Cinch, shake out the reins, and lay them on the rail.
Dapple and white the horses are; perfect they are;
Sneezing to clear their cool black muzzles.

He mounts.

The chariot's basket dips. The whip
Fires in between the horses' ears.
And as in dreams, or at Cape Kennedy, they rise,
Slowly it seems, their chests like royals, yet
Behind them in a double plume the sand curls up,
Is barely dented by their flying hooves,
And wheels that barely touch the world,
And the wind slams shut behind them.

"Fast as you are," Achilles says,
"When twilight makes the armistice,
Take care you don't leave me behind
As you left my Patroclus."

And as it ran the white horse turned its tall face back
And said:
    "Prince,
This time we will, this time we can, but this time cannot last.
And when we leave you, not for dead, but dead,
God will not call us negligent as you have done."

    And Achilles, shaken, says:
"I know I will not make old bones."

And laid his scourge against their racing flanks.

Someone has left a spear stuck in the sand.